What You Need to Know Before You Travel to
CROATIA

Croatia Traveler's Guide to Make the Most Out of Your Trip

~~~

By The Non Fiction Author

Copyright © 2017 by The Non Fiction Author

All Rights Reserved. No part of this publication may be reproduced, distributed, or transmitted in any form or by any means, including photocopying, recording, or other electronic or mechanical methods, without the prior written permission of the publisher, except in the case of brief quotations embodied in critical reviews and certain other noncommercial uses permitted by copyright law. All pictures are held by commercial license and may not be duplicated by anyone without express permission.

Although the author and publisher have made every effort to ensure that the information in this book was correct at press time, the author and publisher do not assume and hereby disclaim any liability to any party for any loss, damage, or disruption caused by errors or omissions, whether such errors or omissions result from negligence, accident, or any other cause.

TABLE OF CONTENTS

Introduction:
Why You Will Fall in Love with Croatia! 6

Chapter 1:
Croatia At a Glance (History, Tips, Currency) 9

Chapter 2:
Croatian Activities You Must Absolutely Do! 14

Chapter 3:
Let's Start At the Beginning - Planning Your Trip 23

Chapter 4:
Where to Sleep (Hotels, Hostels, Tips, & More) 29

Chapter 5:
How to Get Around In Croatia (Without Getting Lost!) 38

Chapter 6:
Travel Tips to Maximize Your Journey 42

Chapter 7:
Crash Guide to Croatia's Best Shopping Stores 51

Chapter 8:
Croatian Beaches You Must Absolutely Go to 55

Chapter 9:
Where to Dine and What to Eat in Croatia 59

Chapter 10:
Zagreb 65

Chapter 11:
Dubrovnik & Southern Dalmatia 69

Chapter 12:
Istria 73

Chapter 13:
Split 77

Chapter 14:
Exploring Some of Croatia's Best Islands 79

Conclusion:
Aren't You Excited? Your Trip Is About to Begin! 82

INTRODUCTION: WHY YOU WILL FALL IN LOVE WITH CROATIA!

"Dobar Dan!" (*"Hello!"* in Croatian)

Croatia has rapidly become one of Europe's most trendy places to visit. However, it still doesn't feel like a tourist country. It's come a long way since it's long fight for independence in the 1990s. If there's an upside to the constant transition, it's in the rich culture footprint that each government has left behind. Venetian palazzos can be seen near Napoleonic forts, Roman columns, early Slavic churches, and Viennese mansions can be found near Socialist Realist sculptures. Croatia's coast has something for everyone, whether you dream of sunbathing on Zlatni Rat beach, partying in uber trendy and glamorous Hvar Town or relaxing in the natural terrain on the island of Mljet. For the history buff, Croatia offers historical landmarks such as Dubrovnik's Old Town or Split's Diocletian's Palace, where the imposing Roman ruins have been repurposed into a bustling area for day and nightlife.

Although Croatia has steadily become commercialized and booming in some cities, their cuisine, wine, and natural beauty offers so much more than the cliché tourist boom. Luckily, the locals of Croatia feel the same, and restrict the tourist industry by focusing more on local businesses, delicacies, and all Croatia has to offer.

Whether you've come to backpack cross-country, surf the beaches, drink a cocktail on the sand, hike the waterfalls, or see some of the architecture, Croatia has a little something for everyone. Croatia's gorgeous beaches, rocky shores, islands, and several National Parks make every picture a potential postcard perfect shot. With over 1,200 islands, turquoise waters, and villages that step out of a fairy tale, it's easy to see why Croatia's tourism is rapidly growing year after year. Away from the coast you can explore the oasis of Plitvice Lakes, hike and climb in the dramatic mountains of Paklenica or spot rare exotic birds and wildlife at Kopački Rit wetlands. It's also a land of vineyards, with more than 300 geographically defined wine districts. Known for it's "niche festivals", Croatia's tourism offers a unique opportunity to live like a local. These festivals are often featured in random places (think art festivals on the beach, culinary festivals in an abandoned warehouse, or small town music festivals).

If you're looking for some city life and nightlife, Croatia has that available too. From swanky hotels, fancy cocktails, and urban dance floors, Croatia has an appeal for any taste. Speaking of taste, Croatia's restaurant culture is as diverse as the country itself. Though Croats traditionally see themselves as a Western country with its close proximity to Italy, many of the landmarks and food staples in Croatia resemble Balkan culture. Croatia offers fresh seafood from the Adriatic Sea, homemade delicacies such as olive oil, wine, cheese, and don't forget sampling rakia!

HERE'S A QUICK RUNDOWN OF OUR GUIDE FOR EASY REFERENCE.

- Chapter 1: A brief overview of Croatia-Historical knowledge on its lengthy battle to become independent and the road to becoming one of Europe's trendiest countries to visit.

- Chapter 2 – Essential Croatia Experiences: A brief "To Do" list of Croatia's top attractions from a visitor's perspective, helping you to narrow down your list and help set your itinerary.

- Chapter 3 – Essential Croatia Travel Planning: This chapter starts with a rundown of the best of Croatia, important things to consider when planning your trip, and a "To Do" list of top attractions. Whether looking for historical, famous, sights or preferring adventure with the unknown attractions, we have you covered.

- Chapter 4 – Where to Sleep: From hostiles to five star luxuries, Croatia hospitality is just as diverse as the country itself. Whether staying in a penthouse or sleeping on a couch, we have options for every preference. This chapter covers it all and includes what websites to do your research on, and what places to look for specifically.

- Chapter 5 – Transportation in Croatia: From cabs to subways to buses, we have the inside scoop on all you need to know. From airports that travel country wide or international, we have the information on all of Croatia's eight airports.

- Chapter 6 - How to Travel Smart, Experience More, and Spend Less: Croatia is one of Europe's most trendy places to visit. With the increasing tourism, it's hard to know where you are able to cut corners. We've compiled a list of ways to travel smart and stay in budget.

- Chapter 7-Where to Shop-Did someone say shopping? This Chapter provides some of the best places to shop until you drop! From outdoor markets to marble lined streets that will make you feel like you've stepped into a movie, we have your bases covered for any budget!

- Chapter 8-The Best Beaches in Croatia-This Chapter provides some of the best beaches in Croatia. We've also taken out the stress of packing and have you covered with an essential list of what to bring on your beach trip.

- Chapter 9-Where to Dine and What to Eat in Croatia-This Chapter provides some of the places to eat in Croatia as well as expands on local delicacies that you must try!

- Chapters 10-14: These chapters provide an in depth look into Croatia's most famous cities. These chapters provide great tips, details, insights, noteworthy attractions, and hidden gems in each of Croatia's distinguished most distinguished cities. They're packed with local tips of where to eat, drink, party, and how to experience Croatia like a local and off the beaten path.

- Chapter 13: See you in Croatia! A brief conclusion and thank you.

CHAPTER 1: CROATIA AT A GLANCE (HISTORY, TIPS, CURRENCY)

CROATIA'S TRANSITIONAL HISTORY

Located between Balkans and Central Europe, the land of Croatia has been through a lot of transition, to say the least. After being passed between competing kingdoms such as the Roman Empire or the Croats Tribe, they united under the independent name Yugoslavia. After years of bitter fights, Croatia finally declared its independency late in the 20th century.

Although still a relatively new independent country in terms of history and time, Croatia's long journey makes the country rich in diverse culture and its own unique history in architecture. From Venetian palazzos, to Napoleonic forts, to Roman and amphitheaters, as well as intricate Viennese mansions and Socialist Realist sculptures, Croatia's transitional history are apparent in its architecture.

With so much transition of rule and identity, historians today still are unclear with the exact timeline of Croatia's rule. This centrally located country offered extensive trade and migratory opportunities for growing civilization. To fully understand Croatia's complex architecture and long journey to its relatively new independence, you must understand some of the backstory to Croatia. Here are a couple important periods in Croatian history:

THE ROMAN EMPIRE PERIOD

From about 11 B.C. to about the 5th century A.D., the Romans dominated most of Western and Eastern Europe. During this era, the territory of what is now modern Croatia was organized into two specific areas. The coastal area called was Dalmatia while the northern area was known as Pannonia. The Romans, known for their strong trade routes and advanced roads, linked the Aegean and Black Seas with the Dalmatian coast. This provided ample trade and commerce opportunities within the Roman Empire. While little is left of the Roman Empire in Croatia, the amphitheater in Pula is still standing and a footprint of the past historical significance. For those able to stop for a visit in Pula, make sure to compare the Roman's grander amphitheater of the Coliseum in Rome. Although a much smaller version, both pieces of architecture have similar artistic qualities as well as materials. The Romans must have done something right for both to be free standing over 2000 years and going!

THE CROAT TRIBES

While the Roman Empire was highly advanced in areas of trade and internal empire improvements such as their expansive roads, they lacked knowing how to live within their means. As their empire expanded, they had a hard time ruling their empire as tightly as they could before. Soon, a Slavic tribe called the Croats migrated to Croatia and formed permanent homes and communities within the country. Although historically unclear on the exact date, it is estimated that by the middle of the 7th century, the Croat tribes migrated into Pannonia and Dalmatia, and powerful clans and rulers emerged from the Roman Empire's ruins.

THE CHRISTIANITY SPREADS

In 800 A.D., Charles the Great, both Frankish emperor and ruler of Western Europe conquered Dalmatia and launched a campaign to convert Croat citizens and rulers to Charles' religion Christianity. After Charles's empire ended, the

Byzantine Empire took control over most of Dalmatia, while the Pannonian Croats remained under Frankish rule. Charles' focus on the conversion of Christianity lasted long after his rule. The Catholic faith strengthened cultural ties with Rome, which later helped in Croatia's foundation of their national identity. Today, the majority of Croats (about 90%) are still Catholic.

MEDIEVAL TIMES

In a time of unsettled serfdom, lords, and knights, Croatia looked for a steady ruler. Beginning in 925, Croatia the Kingdom was officially born. The Kingdom united Dalmatia and Pannonia into one single kingdom. During this time due to location and the united force, Croatia became one of the most powerful forces in the Balkans. After King Tomislav, ruler of Croatia the Kingdom's death, his royal successors continued to rule the kingdom until the end of the 11th century, when Hungary took control.

Land=Power

When Hungary took control of Croatia, King Ladislaus of Hungary became the new ruler of Croatia. As the Ottoman Empire tried to seize control of the, Croatia joined the Hapsburgs empire and fell under the reign of the Austro-Hungarian Empire. After the end of World War I in 1918, Croatia joined forces with the Serbs and formed the official "Kingdom of Serbs, Croats, and Slovenes" aka the "Kingdom of Yugoslavia". This kingdom was a huge disaster and declined rapidly. Other opposing groups saw the declining kingdom and tried to seize control in the opportunity. Croats were brutally murdered and the country was terrorized. The Partisans, another group, took control of Yugoslavia.

In 1980 the cracks in the Partisan's rule lead to a weak economy and a weak government. Croatia finally declared independence from Yugoslavia on June

25, 1991, a day that is now known and celebrated as "Statehood Day." At that same time, Serbs resisting the independence living in the Krajina proclaimed cession from Croatia, which lead to a brutal four-year Civil War.

THEN TO NOW: MODERN CROATIA

It has been two full decades since the end of war in Croatia and their fight for independence. Today, the local population is roughly 4.28 million, roughly half of the population of New York City. The capital city is Zagreb, although one of the most popular cities is Dubrovnik. The country joined NATO in Spring 2009 and finally joined the European Union in July 2013. Since then, the economy has continued to hold strong with stabilized government and a steady flow of tourism. Gone are the memories of unsettled politics. A thriving economy, sapphire waters, romantic historic towns, and delicious local delicacies now place those painful memories.

IMPORTANT INFORMATION ABOUT CROATIA

Currency: Kuna

Visas: Generally not required but last up to 90 days

Busiest Tourist Season: Summer

Electricity: 230V/50hz

Climate: The weather is diverse as Croatia's terrain. The Mediterranean areas on the coast with mild, wet winters, an early spring and autumn and hot, dry summers. The continental inland, with cold winters and hot summers. In Zagreb, temperatures average 35C (80F) in July, falling to 2C (35F) in January.

The Country Flag: The Croatian flag of Croatia in December 1990 (Six months before Croatia officially proclaimed independence from Yugoslavia). The red, white and blue colors that are used in the flags of several Slavic countries have been used in the Croatian flag since 1848. A Coat of arms is set in the center of the flag.

Croatian Anthem: The national anthem of Croatia is "Ljepa nasa domovino" which translates to English as "Our Beautiful Homeland".

Internet/Wifi: Like many other countries today, wi-fi in Croatia is continually improving all the time. If you do not opt for an international plan during your travels, you can at least find least one wi-fi network wherever you are. Some towns (or parts of towns) are even setting up their own free-to-use hotspots. More and more hotels or accommodation places (particularly private room hotels accommodation) offer complimentary wi-fi for their guests.

Traveler Tip: Make sure to get a calling card or a travel app like What's App or Skype to be able to contact relatives or friends back home.

CHAPTER 2: CROATIAN ACTIVITIES YOU MUST ABSOLUTELY DO!

As any true Croat will tell you, there's no way to see all the highlights of this vast, complex country in just one visit. That's part of the thrill of traveling to a new country is that there's always something new to discover. From iconic landmarks to local favorites these essentials must be at the top of your list. We've compiled a list of ways you not only can spot true Croat, outside of their habitat, but can blend in with the locals.

WAYS TO SPOT A TRUE CROAT IN CROATIA OR HOW TO ACT WITH ONE:

Practice living like a Dalmatian

'Fjaka' (pronounced "fyaka") means "the relaxed like". To have the mindset and lifestyle of fjaka is a way of life in Dalmatia and is something that cannot be taught, but something the Dalmations think is something you can feel. To act like a true Dalmation, practice the art of relaxation. It seems easier than it looks! Let your mind go, release the stress, and remember you are in Croatia to travel and

They're Bicycling or Scooting Their Way Somewhere. Typically, they do not rent a taxi.

If you plan on living like a Dalmatian and trying the "relaxed life", then leave the stress of being stuck in a taxi at home. Enjoy the natural beauty of Croatia by driving a scooter or renting a bike through the hillsides. Head to Istria to enjoy a bike tour through wine country, and stop to have an antipasto and glass of wine. Enjoying life in Croatia is to live life.

They always have a cup of coffee in hand or are at the cafe.

Croatians love their coffee or "kava". To live in full "relaxed life" mode like a Croatian, try to drink a single cup of coffee slowly sipping at it for hours while watching the world pass on by. Croatians are infatuated with their coffee culture. Full bodied, rich, whipped, with cream, or without, cafes are often busy and filled with Croatians enjoying their time conversing over coffee. To act like a true Croatian, you must keep the caffeine intake continuous.

Eat breakfast like a local

Dalmatians enjoy most meals similar to a Balkan or Mediterranean lifestyle. Dalmatia Brunch is called "Marenda". Marenda usually consists of seasonal fruits and vegetables, nuts (such as almonds), fresh meats, seafood, cheese, and fresh brandy.

Wear Sunglasses

Croatians live a relaxed lifestyle and what better way to show off their "European cool" than to wear sunglasses. Dalmatians usually have two pairs of sunglasses: a less expensive pair for use at the beach and sunbathing, and a more expensive chic pair when walking around the city. 'Cvike' pron- svi-ke is the local coastal slang for sunglasses, and they are the must have accessory for Dalmatians. So make like the Dalmatians and wear your sunglasses!

CROATIA HIGHLIGHTS

There is so much to do in Croatia. Whether you're looking for adventure, living like a local, or getting down on a dance floor, the diverse history and people of Croatia make the country a paradise of variety. Get a taste of the country with top highlights, ranging from historical to mouthwatering, famous, and the unusual.

Hvar: the Town-For those looking for a vacation spot like St. Tropez while still rocking a travel budget, the town of Hvar is the place to be. Whether looking for mixology cocktail bars, local delicacies, or dancing the night way, the town of Hvar offers a diverse cultural experience. Locals compare Hvar the Town to the luxury beach town of Ibizia.

Skradinski buk -The Krka National Park is a natural gem. The park provides hiking trails and a stunning series of waterfalls. Don't forget to take your bathing suit and water shoes, as the rocks tend to be sharp.

Trsteno -Travel just north of Dubrovnik to the breathtaking Renaissance gardens in this beautiful coastal village. Capture the artistic beauty and relax with the scenery. We recommend bringing close toed walking shoes for this trip, as walking is a must.

Hvar: The Remote Island-If looking to get away from the hustle of metropolitan life and in search of a digital detox, we recommend the untouched natural island of Hvar. Offering reclusive bays and coves, the island offers a natural getaway.

Istria –This area of Croatia has been called "the new Tuscany" and it's not hard to see why. There are brightly hilltop villages, seaside towns and its Italian neighbors inspire food.

Sunsets in Zadar -Alfred Hitchcock said there wasn't a sunset anywhere else like one in Zadar. Make sure to listen and look for the sound-and-light effects of the famous Greeting to the Sun and Sea Organ art installations.

The Elaphite Islands -These gorgeous islands are easy to explore and offer great hiking, swimming, sandy beaches for sunbathing, and plenty of tranquility.

Stari Grad –Feel transported back to medieval times to Stari Grad, where you can find scenic stone houses and Renaissance palaces in one of the more quiet towns on the Dalmatian coast.

The Premužic Trail- Croatia's most exhilarating long-distance hiking route takes in mountain ridges, dense forests and awesome views.

Pelješac peninsula-Explore the rocky mountain scenery, quiet coves and low-key seaside villages in a region renowned for its fantastic and complex red wines and fresh seafood.

Cafe culture, Zagreb-One of the nicest ways to experience špica, the Saturday morning and pre-lunch coffee drinking ritual, is on a terrace in Zagreb. Order your coffee like a true Croat and relaxed while people watching.

Walk around the Old Town in Dubrovnik. Dubrovnik is one of the top cities to visit, with all there is to do and it's natural beauty. It's packed with five star luxury hotels, decadent dishes from upscale restaurants and countless tourists. If you stay away from the main touristy streets, you'll find a whole different world.

NOTEWORTHY MUSEUMS

Museum of Contemporary Art, Zagreb –Known for its trendy and modern city culture, Zagreb has recently become recognized as a strong forefront of European arts and culture. The new building facility hosts local and international artists.

Pula Amphitheater, Pula-During the Roman Empire's rule of Croatia, the Pula Amphitheater was built in their architecture and style. Much like their much bigger brother the Coliseum in Rome, this amphitheater is still standing. To make it even more awesome, the venue is still accessible to the public and used as a venue in the summer for concerts and plays.

Pazin's Kaštel, Istria- Feel like you've stepped back into the Medieval times as Pazin's Kaštel is the largest and best-preserved medieval structure in Istria. Its architecture has hints of design inspiration from Romanesque, Gothic and Renaissance architecture. Historians believe the structure was built somewhere around 1000 A.D. Today, Pazin's Kašte has two museums inside; one that contains an exhibition about slave revolts, and torture instruments in the dungeon. The other museum has roughly 4200 artifacts portraying traditional Istrian village life, including garments, tools and pottery.

The Museum of Broken Relationships-This museum is unique because it doesn't cater or tell the story of anyone famous, but more so of those who are looking for closure in life that they may have never received. Individuals from around the world donate items that remind them of lost love along with the story that explains the item's significance. https://brokenships.com/

Visit the historical site- Six historical sites are official UNESCO World Heritage sites: old city of Dubrovnik, historic city of Trogir, historical complex of Split, the Cathedral of St James in Sibenik, Episcopal Complex of the Euphrasian Basilica in Porec, and Stari grad plains. Each of them is worth visiting and exploring.

Museum of Contemporary Art, Zagreb: Seen as the most significant museum to open in Zagreb in more than a century.

Archeological Museum, Split-Located next to the National Theater, the Archeological Museum offers key historical discoveries that unlock our history's past. Release your inner history buff and view relics of past civilizations such as mosaics and paintings.

Greta Gallery- Centrally located and constantly transitioning, Gallery Greta is one of the more popular attractions in Zagreb. A new exhibition opens every Monday.

Maritime Museum, Dubrovnik- St. John's Fortress initially guarded the entrance of the old harbor. The museum's exhibits include model ships, sailors' uniforms, navigational equipment, flags and maps.

IMPORTANT FESTIVALS TO TRY TO ATTEND

June: *Zagreb*: Eurokaz European theatre festival.

July: *Zagreb*: International Folklore Festival, with embroidery, dancing and song.

End of August to May: *Zagreb* or *Split*: Since the national football team beat Germany in 1998, any game at Dinamo (Zagreb) or Hajduk (Split) is worth watching

Mid-October: *Zagreb*: International Days of Jazz; one of Croatia's many music based and jazz festivals.

ACTIVITIES GALORE!

The saying goes "when in Rome, do as the Romans do." Well, Croatia and Italy aren't so far apart! The best way to truly experience a culture while vacation is to dive into the same activities that the locals do. These activities are hidden gems among tourist activities, showing you sites like locals love to see while satisfying everyone is your party.

- **Glavani Park, Barban** – This is a great family activity that's a physical challenge, mental push, and a lot of fun. Travelers and locals alike love this park for it's intricate rope climbing course, it's high swing, ziplines, and it's adventurous nature overall. While completing the challenges, you're also overlooking some of Croatia's most stunning views. Instructors will give you a brief tour and walk to through the process of how to safely conduct each activity. It's truly fun for the whole family.

- **Cave Bisevo, Island Bisevo** – This incredible cave show's off one of nature's most beautiful spectrums of blues. A boat tour is available to travel through the waters into the cave and learn a bit of history along the way. However, boat owners can take their own boats into the cave (as long as it's within the specified parameters). The awe-inspiring experience evokes a mysterious feel and a welcome quiet as your explore each corner of the large creation from nature. Be sure to bring a GoPro or waterproof camera.

- **Diocletian's Palace, Split** – This historic palace is unique in that it's still active today – just reimagined a bit. It's now a microvillage, busy with bars, restaurants, and churches. There's even a hotel in the palace itself. It's a rare fusion of an active, modern town and stepping back in time, with striking architecture and a rich history behind it. Locals love the buzzing activity and it's incredible structure that manages to stay cool on the hottest of days. Travelers love it for it's one-of-a-kind atmosphere and access to modern culture and impressive history at once. Up for a challenge? Try the guided climb and see a view unlike any other. It's worth the sweat!

- **Peek and Poke Museum, Rijeka** – For a little nostalgia trip and a familiar slice of home, this museum offers a great look at the history of computers and gaming. It has Atari, Sega, and all of the Nintendo family on display, and even has some consoles to play on. It's also traces back a variety of computers and even some calculators. The owner is very passionate and hands on, customizing your experience to your interests. It's much more interactive than your typical museum (hence the name). It's a geeky paradise!

- **Kamenjak National Park, Premantura** – The enormous national park is a breathtaking experience for tourists, but locals love it's functionality. The beautiful views of water, mountainous terrain, fields, and cliffs all within the same confines make this park an incredible exploration. The diversity within the square footage is unparalleled. It's a haven for bicyclists and runners, as well as beachgoers who are okay with skipping sand. You can even go cliff diving. There are some bars and restaurants available through the quiet coves and inlets of the park.

- **Visit Plitvice Lakes National Parks**. The park features a series of waterfalls in the oldest national park in Southeast Europe and the largest national park in Croatia

- **Krk Island**-One of Croatia's largest islands also happens to be extremely busy in prime summer months. And there's good reason why: The landscape is extremely diverse, the beaches are pristine and the towns are full of activities.

- Go Snorkeling and Scuba Diving Croatia isn't known for its snorkeling, but it shouldn't be forgotten about. The rocky shores make the sea bed perfect for snorkeling and scuba diving because of its visability. Croatia is known for all of the shipwrecks viewable off shore. There are 8 in situ underwater museums in Croatia with remains of ships and cargo dating back to 1st century BC. Beside shipwrecks from the ancient times, you'll also find lots of war shipwrecks like Baron Gautsch ship wreck off the coast of Rovinj, or Taranto shipwreck near Dubrovnik.

- Go on a wine tour. Croatia has a long history of wine making, with some dating back as far as 2000 years. The diverse land offers a variety of indigenous grape varieties, and lots of geographically defined wine regions. No matter where you travel in Croatia, you'll find wine cellars, tasting and tour opportunities, and sprawling vineyards. Wineries such as Dingač and Postup offer breathtaking views of the sea, while the area of Istria offers delicious Italian style wines.

INFAMOUS PHOTO OPPORTUNITIES

- Sip rakia (a local popular fruit brandy in Croatia) with your pinky out!

- Take a photo in Dubrovnik's "Cave Bar More" beach bar that feature the main bar in an actual cave, and parts of the floor are glass to appear down on a water filled cavern.

- Take a photo at Plitvice Lakes National Parks' tumbling waterfalls and glistening pools of water.

- Travel to the capital of the island of Rab, south of Krk, and view one of the best-preserved medieval town in the northern Adriatic

- Walk the medieval city walls of Dubrovnik and take a picture of the views of the sea and the Old Town.

THE "I CAN'T BELIEVE I JUST DID THAT" CROATIA MOMENT

- Walk the City Walls around the Old Town in Dubrovnik
- Cliff Jump in Dalmatia
- Sit in the Roman amphitheater in Pula
- Eat a Truffle in Istria
- Alfred Hitchcock once said there isn't a better sunset than one in Zadar. Head over to Zadar and experience a sunset with a glass of homemade wine.
- Experience the Rijeka Carnival. It's the second biggest carnival celebration in Europe after Venice
- Visit the Museum of Broken Relationships in Zagreb, Croatia and leave something from an ex
- Try the local Zadar delicacy Pag cheese; made on the small island of Pag near Zadar. There a unique set of weather conditions produces one of the best sheep's milk cheese; especially great when paired with salty prosciutto and some homemade Croatian wine.
- Take the short ferry trip from Split to magical Hvar, the longest of the 1,000 Croatian islands.
- Take the trip to the remote island of Vis and visit The Blue Cave. Located off Bisevo Island on Vis, the Blue Cave is the area's biggest tourist attraction. The blue color of the cave appears when sunlight comes in through a side cave, and it's visible 11 a.m. to noon only on days when the sun shines.
- Rent a Lighthouse apartment (no we're not kidding!) www.lighthouses-croatia.com
- Go Sea Kayaking

CHAPTER 3:
LET'S START AT THE BEGINNING - PLANNING YOUR TRIP

When planning a trip to a country as diverse as Croatia, it should be 75 percent planned and 25 percent completely unplanned. With so many restaurants, shops, bakeries, coffeehouses, and tourism attractions, it would be unfair to the country itself to plan every single minute. Transportation and checking the times for tourist attractions are definitely a must, but you should also plan time to not rush your plans! Make sure to take time to fully wing it and just walk the streets of busier coastal cities. Sit in a park and people watch. Or, take a minute and enjoy Croatia's most beautiful natural places, such as the untouched natural island of Hvar. Offering reclusive bays and coves, the island offers a natural getaway, and you'll be glad that you took a minute to take it all in!

FIRST, GET IT TOGETHER AND GET ORIENTATED

Once you have your itinerary set, make your way to a park or your hotel accommodations for free Wi-Fi. Be sure to download the Yelp, Skype, Airbnb, or WhatsApp apps to stay on top of your travel plans and communicate with family. We've compiled a list of the best travel apps to use when you're traveling overseas. These apps could make your journey a little faster, efficient, cheaper, and smarter.

- **Uber**-If you don't feel like waiting for a cab or taking the subway, you can schedule a ride with your GPS from where you are. The Uber may be slightly pricier than a cab, but it's worth it especially if you're in a time crunch or are in rush hour.

- **Yelp**-When browsing for restaurants, it's best to take the suggestions of locals. Instead of asking, why not use an app to just show you the ratings of the best restaurants in the shortest distance? Yelp is one of the most commonly used apps in New York and it's free!

- **WhatsApp**-Be able to connect with friends and family through the What's App app. Using Wifi, you'll be able to communicate with friends and family back home through a text messaging like service. You even have an option to send photos.

- **Skype**-Be able to connect with friends and family through Skype. Using Wifi, you'll be able to communicate with friends and family back home through phone, video, or messaging service. Bypass expensive international calling fees, which routes calls over a Wi-Fi network for $.02 a minute. If you place calls to other Skype accounts, the call is free of charge.

- **Hopper** (https://goo.gl/xBfsbU)- Planning on taking an impromptu flight? Hopper predicts the best and cheapest time tp buy a flight by analyzing billions of airfares daily and picking out those brief moments when a price drops. Travelers with flexible travel dates have the option to use Hopper's color-coded calendar to spot the best and cheapest dates in a month. Hopper is extremely user friendly and features a "Watch a Flight," option that sends a push notification when the price of a given route decreases.

- **TripAdvisor**- TripAdvisor helps rank restaurants, bars, hotels and sights on a five star system that is completely rated by users. They've also compiled informative lists of the city's must see attractions. The lists constantly change as the ratings fluctuate. For more curated travel tips, TripAdvisor also offers a standalone Offline City Guides app with the most up to date maps that you can download and access later without a mobile data connection.

- **Airbnb**-. Rental options range in a variety of accommodations. From tree houses to vans to renting a room or a flat, Airbnb caters to the continually growing supply of apartments, rooms and sofas to accommodate just about anyone's budget. The app requires a little more administrative work than the typical hotel booking — you'll need to authenticate your identity before you travel and have time to figure out the logistics.

- **Google Translate**-The Google Translate (https://goo.gl/YdyDzY) team created the ultimate user-friendly experience for international travelers: "Conversation mode." All you have to do is open the app, hold the mobile device between two people speaking a different language, and listen as it translates a conversation live. The speakers may struggle to adjust to the lag time and a fair amount of mistranslations, but it absolutely helps with the language barrier.

IMPORTANT TIPS:

- Know where you're losing the clothes. As the typical European comfortability, Croatia offers plenty of beach opportunities for travelers to sunbathe topless on beaches in northern and central Croatia. In some areas, nude beaches prevail. However, make sure you know where you're stripping down! Certain Croatian islands such as the island of Vrbnik, you might find yourself in a bit of trouble! The island of Vrbnik is known as the birthplace of numerous Croatian bishops and a very religious community, so make sure your clothes stay on, as well as research clothing rules (such as making sure your shoulders are covered in religious places of worship).

- Do not walk the walls during peak tourist times! If planning to visit Croatia during peak summer times (June to late August), one of the top tourist attractions is to visit Dubrovnik and walk along the top of the famous City Walls. The City Walls span over 1.6 km around the Old Town of Dubrovnik. These medieval gothic stonewalls were built in the Middle Ages, and still remain a sense of protection and country pride for the Croats. Walking the stonewalls should be on your list of things "to do", but try to visit during the mornings or before sunset in order to avoid getting stuck on dry summer afternoons when it can be crowded and have little mobility.

- While planning your trips, be sure to tack on time to your commute. With public transportation stops, walking to and from ferry/bus stop, as well as potentially getting lost, it's more likely to take more time than less. Also, if you're not familiar with the language, it's a lot harder to read the signs! Be sure to bring a guidebook and map of your own language for easier commuting.

- Never show your wallet or money in public. Always be careful to conceal it. No matter how safe the area, Croatia still has petty thieves who are looking to pawn on unsuspecting tourists. For the busier months, with more population comes more crime. Think smart and you'll be fine!

- Watch your footing! For the adventurous, heading off the beaten path can be appealing. However, if you don't know where you are going, you might want to get a tour guide or talk to the locals, or it may cost your life. Croatia is know for their unexploded minefields in inland areas like Eastern Slavonia, Brodsko-Posavska County, Karlovac County, areas around Zadar County and in more remote areas of the Plitvice Lakes National Park. In the early 1990s, nearly 2 million mines were laid during the war of independence. Due to the extensive implantation of landmines, the Croats have spent tedious years and time extracting these mines carefully. However, Croatia is not expected to be mine-free until 2019. Although these unexploded mines are not in tourist spots, its important to know where you are exploring just to avoid any chance! Although the chances are extremely slim, mines in Croatia have killed hundreds of people after the war. Important tip: keep an eye out for warning signs with the international symbol for mines -- a skull and crossbones inside a red, upside-down triangle.

CROATIA THROUGH THE SEASONS: WHEN TO GO AND WHAT TO EXPECT

Due to its location, Croatia's climate can be broken down into two seasonal patterns: The coastal Mediterranean weather that offers warm breezy summers and mild winters, and the inland area (often called the continental), which due to its distance from the ocean offers slightly hotter temperatures during the summer, and extremely cold temperatures in winter. Croatia splits their seasons into three specific categories: Low Season (October to April), Shoulder (May-June, September), and High Season (July-August).

- **Winter (December to late February)**: Outside of Christmas and New Year, this is the quietest time to visit. The continental area can see frigid winters, with average daily temperatures reaching freezing and unpleasant temperatures December through February. For those unaccustomed to a "true winter" we recommend you travel on the more temperate months. From October to May the coastal popular tourist areas can be very quiet, as many hotels and tourist attractions close down for the winter. We recommend heading to historical areas like Zadar, Split, or Dubrovnik, which can offer milder winter temperatures and low tourist lines. Many hotels that remain open have reduced rates due to the slower season, with prices as low as fifty percent less than peak season! Holiday season brings buzz to the streets, even with the snow, plus there's skiing too.

- **Spring (mid to late March to early May)**: Spring is one of the shortest seasons in Croatia's inland, but the Mediterranean coastal area can have spring weather until the end of June. If trying to stay away from the tourist peak season of summer, we highly recommend visiting in the spring. The warm, drier weather makes this season a great time to do outdoor activities such as cycling, hiking, or touring many of the historical sights when they aren't packed with tourists. The coastal areas tend to drop temperatures as the sunsets, so be prepared to bring a medium weight jacket and longer pants. It's still too cold to swim along the coastal areas, so be prepared. The coast is gorgeous; the Adriatic Sea is usually warm enough for swimming or at least light water sports. The crowds are a lot less and prices are lower. In spring and early summer, the steady maestral wind makes sailing, windsurfing, and other wind sports great.

- **Summer (Middle May/June to late August)**: Because school is out, summer in Croatia is peak season for families and tourists. Be prepared to fight the swarming crowds. July and August are the peak season for tourism along the coastal Mediterranean, when the area becomes packed with locals, things to do, and nightlife extends its hours. The summer season daytime temperatures can be hot and sometimes unbearable for both the inland and costal areas. However, if you're looking for prime beach weather and ample nightlife opportunities, then the summertime is when you need to go! Make a trip to Southern Dalmatia for warmer waters and breathtaking views. If looking to tour Croatia in the summer months, plan ahead! Hotel accommodations fill up fast, the prices are higher, and the area stays busy until late August.

- **Autumn (early September to early December)**: Due to the Mediterranean coastal weather, fall is Croatia's longest season. As schools become back in session, the crowds for popular tourist sites tend to die down. The days are still warm, the weather is still pleasant, and the humidity (as well as hotel peak prices) has waned down. We love Autumn in Croatia! Like the springtime, Autumn is a good time to enjoy all things outdoors such as the inland Istria and national park areas like the Plitvice Lakes and the River Krka. During autumn, the leaves are changing and a cooler breeze keeps walking around in the daytime pleasant.

CHAPTER 4:
WHERE TO SLEEP (HOTELS, HOSTELS, TIPS, & MORE)

This guide only lists well-recommended accommodations. Be sure to do your research and take the tips into consideration before purchasing.

PROXIMITY TO PUBLIC TRANSPORTATION

Most hotels will advertise that they are in close proximity to bars, shops, and attractions. The lower the price, the lesser the truth behind that statement. The most important things a tourist should look at is the close proximity to where they want to go, the ratings and comments from past travelers, and the actual distance from public transit. Croatia offers public transportation in a variety of their cities. From ferries to trams to buses, make sure to inquire about a transportation map online before traveling. Read the reviews and call the hotel for any questions before you book. You can purchase a stay at a breathtaking water's edge hotel, but that won't do you very well if you're traveling in the winter, have to walk in the frigid cold long distances, and aren't sure what restaurants are open on the off season. Think about location!

YOU DON'T HAVE TO SELL YOUR KIDNEY TO FIND A GREAT HOTEL

Staying somewhere off the beaten track is exciting and always makes for a good story! As we've said before, the farther away you move from popular tourist attractions, the cheaper the price will be. The further you get from the water, the cheaper the price will be (because you have to walk further to see gorgeous sea views). If you're planning to have an active nightlife and don't want to walk (or want to wear a pair of killer heels) keep in mind that taxis can add up and add up quick. If you're willing to compensate a less expensive hotel for more money in cab rides, then by all means do your research!

TAKE ADVANTAGE OF HOTEL DEALS

From Travelzoo to Hotwire to Groupon to Kayak, there are enough travel sites to give you whiplash. When looking at hotels, do your research and find the best deal. Websites such as Priceline.com offer refunds if you find a cheaper price. Hotwire offer's "Hotel Roulette" which means you pay the price, find the area, and they'll match you with a hotel of that value or greater. If you've seen a deal that may have expired, call the hotel and ask them to extend the offer. You'll be surprised how many will be accommodating! Do your research and you'll be happy to save the extra $$$

CONSIDER A FLIGHT/HOTEL COMBO OR PACKAGE.

If you need at least three-star comfort from your hotel, you should check out the deals offered by package operators. From the UK, it's hard to beat Jet2Holidays. From North America, try BookingWIZ which compares results from Orbitz, Expedia, Travelocity, CheapTickets and Priceline to get the best fares.

BUDGET, BUDGET BUDGET

Yes, it may be your vacation, but budgeting cannot hurt. When people think of Croatia, they think of the posh beach locations with pool boys and tented cabanas. Let's be realistic. Most locals don't live like that, and most hotels don't have rooms like those unless you're willing to spend the big bucks. Lower your expectations and plan your budget. If you don't have a view, don't sweat it! Many hotels offer rooftop bars so you can get those sprawling views of the city. Save a little and you'll be glad when you did when you get your dinner bill.

TRAVEL OFF-SEASON AND SPLURGE A LITTLE.

Prices are at their peak in July and August due to the increase of tourism and travel. After the peak season, they fall off rapidly before. Everything costs more during the summer season from accommodation to ferry prices to car rentals. Plus, Croatia is great in spring and autumn! Even if you travel to Croatia in the winter, you can get great deals on spas and wellness centers.

ARRANGE FOUR-NIGHT STAYS OR LONGER.

Owners of private accommodations in Croatia tend to drop the prices the longer you stay. Many impose a 30% surcharge on short stays, which help them pay for added costs of the extra cleaning and laundry for short-term clients.

ACCOMMODATION OPTIONS AND LISTINGS

Hotels and hostels compete with each other in the "dog eat dog" environment, so your options will be distinctly different and hard to choose. Rather than being stuck with hundreds of options, and no idea where to go in a foreign city, this guidebook offers you a variety of accommodations for any preference. From "Dorm-like" hostels to 5 star hotels, we give you a little piece of everything.

If you're planning on booking a trip in the Summer (June to August) months, expect prices to go up due to inflation and popularity. If you're looking to head to the Adriatic or coastal fronts, try off season months in the Spring or Fall when the weather is warm but the prices are reasonable. Most budget and mid-range accommodations in Croatia are still in the form of private rooms and apartments, and there has been an explosion in the number of backpacker-friendly hostel-type establishments in the major cities.

HOSTELS AND BUDGET HOTELS

Before the Internet, hostels and budget hotels had a bad reputation. They were seen as unsafe travel accommodations, and tourists traveling especially from a different country were warned of possible theft or danger. Today, hostels and the hospitality environment have seen a vast improvement in hotels, hostels, and other accommodations. Hostels are great traveling options for the traveler on a budget. Hostels continue to be the most affordable lodging option in the city, and with the constant competition of reasonable hotels and apartment sharing websites; they've started to up their game with modern amenities such as free Wi-Fi. If you don't mind sharing a room with a stranger (or new friend, depending on how you look at it) hostels can be a great and affordable option. Many hostels also offer locker and safe options so that you won't have to worry about your belongings when you're out on the town.

Dubrovnik's Villa Divine –located forty meters from the sea, Villa Divine is a slice of heaven at a fraction of the cost. This hostel is in a safe and great location 10 minutes away from the main beach in Dubrovnik. Linens, towels, Free Wifi and washing machines are included to make you feel right at home. https://goo.gl/P1GdoF

Zagreb's Taban Hostel- Located in one of Zagreb's most popular streets, Tkalčićeva, Taban Hostel offers a café bar on site that often has live music and a terrace where guests can have a drink and view the bustling street below. Hostels offer fridges, private bathrooms, lockers, and linens give you all the amenities you need while traveling. https://goo.gl/r58N5a

Istria's Hostel Papalinna-This airy hotel overlooks the seaside with cheap and stylish rooms. Lockers, linens, and towels are complimentary, as well as a 24 hour receptionist to help you with any travel questions.

Dubrovnik's Prijeko Palace-Located in the Old Town of Dubrovnik, Prijeko Palace offers air conditioned individual accommodations, free wifi, and easy access to some of Dubrovnik's landmarks and activities. https://goo.gl/FULtNE

Hotel Priscapac Resort & Apartments- Hotel Priščapac Resor & Apartments is located in Prizba on the island of Korcula. Located right on the beach, it's a surprisingly affordable retreat from the busier city life and offers in house restaurants on site.

Silver Central Hostel, Split-The boutique hostel offers dorm rooms, a lounge area, as well as complimentary airport transfers.

West Coast Rooms, Split-This trendy and airy hotel offers complimentary linens, toiletries, and Wifi. It's walking distance from the Palace of Diocletian and the Cathedral of St. Domninus.

CROATIA'S BEST HOTELS

At the crux of any great trip is a great hotel. After a long day of exploring or a relaxing day on the beach, you want to come back to an environment that you trust, and that will enhance your experience rather than detract from it. This list of Croatia's top hotels will provide you with where to stay on the most popular islands.

- **Hotel Monte Mulini, Ravinj** – This hotel creates the perfect experience for families, couples, and grown up getaways alike. The different tiers of rooms are sure to accommodate whatever about of space you need. The clean, spacious rooms have balconies that overlook the water, overlooking boats in passing and lush greenery. If it's chlorinated water that you're after, the pool is right by the sea, giving you the same stunning view from ground level. The hotel grounds are decorated with gardens, have a bar that's shared with non-residents, and allow you direct access to a restaurant from inside. The staff will also go out of their way to make sure that you feel at home during your stay. The facility and the location balance privacy with activity and adventure.

- **Royal Princess Hotel, Dubrovnik** – The name says it all with this waterside slice of paradise, prompted to make you feel like a princess. Not only is this hotel waterside, but it also boasts four indoor/outdoor swimming pools. The rooms are intimate enough to host couples, but large enough to accommodate large travel groups of up to 30 people. Exploring your branch and the other branches of the resort is enough to preoccupy you, especially with their fully stocked bar, but the beautiful 10 minute walk into town will keep you and your crew in adventure mode.

- **The Esplanade Zagreb Hotel, Zagreb** – The Esplanade Hotel is luxury at it's finest, as expressed through its classy ambiance and indulgent features. Every detail of this hotel is crafted with your best interest in mind, like late check out, bathrooms with heated floors and rain showers (that remember your temperature setting), huge windows, king size beds, an amazing restaurant, and free internet. Its location is also very close to town and the train station, allowing you easy access to your plans.

- **Hotel Trakoscan, Trakoscan** – This hotel blends modern accommodations with stunning views, luxury features, and a very important great night's rest! Their rooms are quiet and spacious, overlooking Croatia's most beautiful terrain with some balconies even facing a castle. The wellness center has a host of relaxing services, like a sauna, Jacuzzi (also with a signature view), and a pool. You can even rent a bike and tour the surrounding lake and castle, a feature unique to this establishment. The modern living is a refreshing stay as the village feels like a historic snapshot.

- **Hotel Luxe, Split** – It's rare to find a central location that's overlooking the sea, but this combination is at the heart of Hotel Luxe. The relaxing, modern rooms overlook the sea, and are surprisingly quiet considering the bustling town is just steps outside of your door. The décor has a colorful European flavor but the updated facility ensures a top-notch stay. The food is delicious, but the location being a huge advantage will have you out and about most of the day while, and feeling safe and pampered upon your return.

- **Aman Sveti Stefan Hotel, Montenegro**-One of the most exclusive 5-star hotels in Croatia, this hotel is located on its own island in a fishing village. It includes 50 rooms and 8 grand suites, the latter at the Villa Milocer, which was once the summer home of Yugoslavia's ruler Queen Maria.

- **Le Méridien Lav, Podstrana**-If staying at a large resort isn't your style of relaxation, the exclusivity of Le Méridien Lav is a luxury hotel to try. This hotel's rooms feature breathtaking views of the Adriatic Sea. The presidential suite is beyond luxurious, with its 2 bedrooms, a dining room and 2 private entrances.

- **La Villa, Dubrovnik**-The small hotel of La Villa lies on the seashore of the Adriatic Sea, overlooking the Dalmatian coast, islands, and nestled in Lopud renaissance harbour. La Villa offers a reasonably priced "get away" experience with style https://goo.gl/edgdf4

- **Palmizana** (https://goo.gl/1QcN3m), **Hvar**-Set in trendy Hvar, Palmizana is the ultimate bohemian getaway, with its eclectic and fresh style. Its bungalows and villas are decorated with bold colors, prints, and modern Croatian art from local artists. Although this getaway is located on island of Palmizana, it only takes a 10-minute boat ride from Hvar town.

MODERN ACCOMMODATION OPTIONS

As technology advances, traveling and personal preferences are constantly changing. People are looking for new and the unusual. Long gone are the days of extreme options on choosing a low budget hostile or a high-end hotel.

Renting someone else's apartment: What says "living like a local" more than actually renting a local New Yorker's apartment. The average New Yorker pays over $1300 a month in rent. If you were traveling and weren't using it, you'd want to compensate too! Innovative companies like Air BnB allow you to rent an apartment safely for both the owner and rentee. Find hosts with extra rooms, entire homes, and unique accommodations such as tree houses, rooftop locations, or closet spaces.

Head over to rent an apartment or room at secure sites like https://goo.gl/gU4Bkp or https://goo.gl/3UeUZa for renting local apartments or a room.

Sleep on a Couch: For the adventurous type, you can sleep on a couch. Couchsurfing offers the options to stay with locals in someone's home and still experience the city. The website connects a social global network of travelers and volunteers for those who want to view different cities, meet new people, and travel on a budget.

Do your research and head to https://goo.gl/VVhMuw to view local Croatian options. We recommend this option best when traveling with a group or at least a buddy!

Rent a lighthouse apartment: No, we're not kidding. Croatia offers the option to have an experience of a lifetime! Located all along the Adriatic Sea, you have the option to pick one of the lighthouses that offer a beautiful view and breathtaking experience. We recommend this when traveling with a group less than 5, as many lighthouses have restrictions to 4 people. www.lighthouses-croatia.com

Rent a fisherman's cottage off the Kornati archipelago: This housing option is another unusual stay option, and we highly recommend thinking outside the box. The Kornati archipelago offers an astounding 89 islands, islets and reefs, which have been designated together as a national park. If you're looking to get away from society and bask in Croatia's natural beauty, the fishermen cottages offer a low-key option to help you get in touch with nature. The national park does not have any fresh water inlets but each cottage offers water from a well, low-voltage solar electricity, and an outdoor shower. https://goo.gl/i2J1sR

Camping on the Beach: Croatia's island like temperatures offer the option to camp on the beach a common substitute instead of a hotel. Simuni Campgrounds can be found in between two sheltered bays on the western shores of Pag Island. Known for its transparent aqua waters, shallow sea depths, and winds, Pag Island is the ultimate retreat for those who enjoy outdoor sports. The weather and temperate conditions make the island idea for activities such as paddle boarding, kayaking, wind surfing, and sailing. Simuni Campgrounds offer an astounding 4,500 guests beds on the beach grounds each day during summertime. It's a prime summer stay accommodation, and offers a lot of great activities such as the campground site's themed evenings and over the top firework displays. If your attention hasn't been caught yet, during the summer months the staff at Simuni offer complimentary roast pork and beer dinners on Wednesdays. If publicly camping with 4,500 people is not your ideal setting, the campgrounds also offer private bungalow and apartment options at a higher but extremely reasonable rate. https://goo.gl/8x435C

CHAPTER 5:
HOW TO GET AROUND IN CROATIA (WITHOUT GETTING LOST!)

A large part of what makes Croatia so beautiful is it's unique topography. As you hop from island to island, you'll find yourself exploring beautiful beaches, bustling city life, and mountainous terrain. The only question is, how do you get there? The diverse landscape does provide a unique challenge, and one that you'll want to make plans around before you book your flight.

BY FERRY

The ferry is one of the most attractive and direct ways to maneuver each island of Croatia. Unlike many destinations, however, there isn't a uniform system and schedule in place. In fact, there is plenty of competition with multiple companies vying for your ticket. Some lines offer car ferries, too. Whatever your needs, you'll want to investigate in advance, and many tickets can be purchased online, saving you chaos and money. Be sure to compare prices, carefully check schedules, and watch out for scammers!

BY BUS

Busses are one of the most efficient and budget friendly ways to explore Croatia. Take advantage of the public transportation! There run frequently on the cheap, and offer multiple routes to the most popular hotspots available. While many bus tours offered to travelers are usually cramped, overcrowded, and uncomfortable, Croatia's are an enjoyable tourists, providing reclining seats and air-conditioning. You don't have to book too far in advance for tickets, but do be aware that seating is assigned and that they run less frequently at night. Buses are reasonably priced, and Croatia's bus companies offer with extensive coverage of the country and frequent departures.

BY TRAIN

If you're looking for a slower paced alternative that connects major cities, a domestic train line is also available. It's not as strongly recommended as it's been under a major overhaul, but the changes are starting to take place as April of 2015 has brought about 44 new trains. Coincidentally, new connections between major cities. Cyclists should note that bikes are permitted on trains as well. While it's not as efficient as other modes of transportation, it is safe and reliable. We'll see what the new changes bring for the future of Croatia's tourism and travel.

Direct rail links with Slovenia, Hungary, Italy, Austria, Switzerland, Slovakia, France, Germany, Bosnia-Herzegovina and Yugoslavia. Indirect rails links with almost all European countries.

BY PLANE

While traveling by ferry is ripe with competition, flying from island to island is not. With most major islands sporting their own airport, the lack of competition keeps flying efficient and streamlined, providing cheap, reliable, and fast flights. Most find the airlines as on par as any other modern one. One quirky tip: Be sure to remove your batteries from you checked luggage!

Today, Croatia has a total of eight main airports that accept international and national flights. Keep in mind; three of these airports only service flights internally so make sure if you are not flying out of the same airport you arrived at, you know which ones. They are located at Zagreb, Rijeka, Split, Dubrovnik, Zadar, Pula, Osijek, and Brac. The main international airport in Croatia is the Zagreb Airport. The airports at Rijeka, Split, Zadar and Dubrovnik serve international flights mainly during the busy tourist summer season.

The national carrier for Croatia, Croatia Airlines, offers a variety of direct flights from London and Manchester to Zagreb, Dubrovnik and Split.

Tip: To explore northern Croatia, it might be cheaper to have a connecting flight outside of the country such as flyingto Venice, then take the train or bus down the coast.

Boats also link Croatia with Italy and Greece; buses connections to major west European cities

ZAGREB INTERNATIONAL AIRPORT

The Zagreb International Airport (also known as Pleso Airport) is located 15 km outside of the city at Pleso. Today it serves more than 2 million passengers a year. With the continuing need for more transportation with tourism growing, it is in process of expansion.

RIJEKA INTERNATIONAL AIRPORT

The airport of Rijeka is located at Omišalj on the Krk island, 17 km away from the city. Transportation options such as bus or taxi services can help you get into the city center without any hassle.

SPLIT INTERNATIONAL AIRPORT

Split International Airport is the second largest in Croatia in terms of served passengers. It is located near Trogir, some 16 km outside Split. During the summer near 1 million tourists fly to Split. Because of that fact there are plans for renovating and expanding the airport. It was opened in 1966 and has continued to grow since then.

DUBROVNIK INTERNATIONAL AIRPORT

Dubrovnik International Airport is also known as Čilipi Airport, and is located at Čilipi, 15 km away from the city. Dubrovnik is one of the main tourist attractions to visit in Croatia. Today, the airport is currently getting a facelift, and has been under construction to hold the increasing number of tourists visiting Croatia. When the construction is done, Dubrovnik International Airport will be the largest terminal in the country. During the summer season, over 1 million passengers(and growing!) enter the country through this airport.

ZADAR INTERNATIONAL AIRPORT

Zadar International Airport is located outside of the city of Zadar. Zadar is small town famous with its gothic architecture and medieval look. Zadar is extremely popular during the summer season, and the airport uses mainly charter flights during this time.

The airports at Pula, Osijek and Brac serve flights only within the borders of Croatia. Look out for inexpensive flights on Croatia Airlines, as it offers transfers to any of the Croatian airports.

CHAPTER 6: TRAVEL TIPS TO MAXIMIZE YOUR JOURNEY

THE ULTIMATE TRAVEL PACK LIST

Before the Travel

International travel is always an exciting adventure, but its hard to know what to prepare for if you've never been there. It's important to be prepared for all situations and travel scenarios. If you are not prepared for travel scenarios, they can quickly turn into potentially dangerous or life threatening situations. From our past experiences, we have put together a travel guide on what to pack and what to prepare for to help you pack for your journey.

One of the biggest things to prepare for in international travel is to always plan that international travel always requires a passport. Most countries also require a visa Visas, which allow you to enter and leave these countries, usually consist of special notations and stamps, which are added to your passport by government officials. Passports take additional time once you have submitted the proper paperwork, so be prepared to plan ahead of your trip to make sure it arrives in time.

Additionally, many countries require immunizations and proof of immunizations for entry into the country. Make sure you should carry your immunization paperwork with you as well as a copy to leave in your suitcase. Meet with your doctor well in advance of your planned departure.

- **Passport with required visas** (passport should be valid for at least six months from start of trip). Get all visas and passport (if expired or you do not have it) in advance.

- **Get all immunizations brought up-to-date in advance.** Make sure to check Croatia's travel requirements before travel.

Items To Not Bring to Croatia and Leave At Home

- Share a copy of your itinerary with a spouse, family, or friend.
- Leave a copy of your passport (photo and visa pages) and other travel documents at home.
- Extra credit cards you will not need.
- I.D. and membership cards (i.e. office cardkey).
- Expensive and religious jewelry.
- Anything that could be viewed as a weapon. Check airport restrictions for proper protocol.

Important Travel Documents To Take With You

- Passport with required visas (make sure your passport should be valid for at least six months from start of trip).
- Visas for entry into countries to be visited, including those in which you will transit.
- Health book or immunization paperwork
- Airline tickets (many countries require round trip ticket for entry).
- Drivers license - State (i.e. Indiana).
- Camera or photo permit
- Traveler checks (exchange for local currency as needed at a bank).
- Major international credit cards (ie. American Express, Diners, and VISA/MasterCard)

- Airline frequent travel cards.

- Telephone numbers at destinations and addresses in countries to be visited - may be needed for landing cards.

- Copy of your passport (photo and visa pages) and other travel documents.

- Paperwork of trip insurance

Travel Medical Insurance

- If you are traveling overseas or away from your home country, you may wish to purchase additional medical insurance for your trip. Your own country's insurance does not work internationally.

- Travel Medical Insurance is very inexpensive and can be a nice item to have in case of emergencies. You have the option to purchase this when you purchase your trip insurance.

Other Necessary Items To Take With You

- Prescription medicines in clearly labeled containers.

- Small first aid kit of some essentials (bandaids, ibuprofen, cold medicine, and antibiotic ointment).

- Medical notes listing allergies and medical conditions.

- Foreign language/English pocket dictionary.

- Alarm clock, battery or wind-up.

- International electronic adapters for electrical items

- Personal appliances (hair dryer, etc.)

Before Departure and at The Airport Tips

- Count your cash before leaving.

- Get export papers from US Customs for computers, video cameras, etc. to make US Customs clearance easier when you return.

- Check in early and go through security immediately.

- Make sure all toiletries follow airport guidelines

Arrival At Destination

- Reconfirm your future flights - local office may be able to assist.

- Exchange a small amount of US dollars for local currency at the airport for taxi, tips, etc. You will usually get a better exchange rate at a bank.

- Know who will meet you or what transportation to take to get to your destination

- Request room above ground floor but not too high.

- Check for exits and emergency instructions.

- Always put valuables in the security boxes.

When Traveling Through the City

- Always stay sober, alert and inconspicuous.

- Stay alert and aware of your surroundings.

- Keep an eye on your drink at all times.

- Keep phone numbers of local contacts with you.

- Keep your money out of sight - never count it in public.

- Find out where the "wrong" parts of town are and stay away.

- Find out the location of the police stations and get phone numbers.

- Avoid disturbances - go the other way, immediately.

- Learn to operate the telephones the first day.

- Always carry your passport, leave copy in security box -- unless local customs require otherwise.
- Don't stop to investigate accidents.
- If accosted try to stay calm, watch for escape.
- If being followed go directly to the police, hotel, or office.

GENERAL COMMENTS AND TIPS

- **Obey all laws of the country you are in - no drugs - no smuggling.**
- **Baggage** - Most airlines allow two bags (max. 70 pounds each -- some size restrictions apply) for direct travel to and from the USA.
- **Check bags** to your final destination.
- Know what you are hand carrying for someone else.
- **Cash** - Many countries require that you declare all of the cash (sometimes traveler checks as well) which you are bringing into the country.
- **Travel Documents** - Check all travel documents before leaving to ensure that they are valid for the duration of your trip, including extensions.
- **Airline Tickets** - Check your airline tickets to ensure that routing is as planned and that you know ALL of your stops.
- **Packing Hints** - The clothing you pack should always be appropriate for the climate and activities on your itinerary. In general, pack:
  - » Clothing that is wrinkle-resistant, drip-dry and comfortable.
  - » Comfortable walking shoes.
  - » Versatile styles that can go from casual to dressy.
  - » Toiletries in unbreakable plastic bottles.

- » Include soap and washcloth.
- » Pack in your carry-on bag
  - An all-weather coat - Europe can be cool anytime of the year.
  - A supply of any medication and extra pair of prescription glasses or contacts lenses.
  - A change of clothing.
  - Duplicate suitcase keys.
- Familiarize yourself with the currency and exchange laws of the countries you plan to visit.
- Tape your name, address, and copy of your passport inside your suitcases.
- Download a foreign currency app to help with your conversion
- Take prescription slips for any necessary medication and eyeglasses.
- Carry a small notebook with your camera to record where photos were taken. Most countries prohibit photographing military and governmental facilities.
- Keep sales receipts handy for customs.
- Most visas are valid for 30 to 90 days from issue - check validity with your schedule.
- Many airports require payment of an airport exit tax - be sure you have the correct amount in the correct currency.
- Many hotel porters require a "verification of payment" slip before they will carry your bags out of the hotel. Ask for this slip from the cashier when you check out.

BUDGETING

Everyone that travels on vacation should have a budget. A budget keeps you on track for what you want to spend, and keeps you in your means so you don't have to hide from the credit card bill at the end of the month. Plan ahead that larger cities like Dubrovnik and Zagreb are the most expensive cities while Hvar is the most expensive island. The villages around Dubrovnik are not that far away and cheaper than Dubrovnik. Jelsa is cheaper than Hvar Town.

Visiting the less touristy regions can save money with more experience and give you more of a "local feel". Before you travel, research places that fall under the tourist radar. We suggest places like Karlovac, Paklenica National Park, Kopacki Rit Nature Park, Cres Island, Vis Island, Pag Island or Dugi Otok. Or visit the islands of the Sibenik archipelago.

FREE DOESN'T MEAN YOU'RE CHEAP

Many of Croatia's most famous attractions are completely free or offer you the option to "Pay What You Can". Obviously, that rule applies to the honor system; so do pay what you are able to.

FREE THINGS TO DO IN CROATIA:

- **Beaches and Lakes**- Most of Croatia's beaches do not charge you a fee for enjoying their beaches. Just make sure not to litter, or you will be paying fees! If staying in Zagreb, head to Jarun Lake, where the sandy beaches are ideal for swimming and sunbathing, and special areas are reserved for wind-surfers, pedalo boats and canoes. Zagreb's Bundek Lake also offers free swimming during the warmer months, as well as with free live entertainment held on its summer performance stage.
- **Mount Srd**-Possibly the best way to appreciate Dubrovnki's large assortment of historical architecture is from above. Standing tall at

413 metres, Mount Srd offers amazing panoramic views and a bit of exercise for those climbing it. If you're not interested in the hour and a half climb, take the cable car that will have you up the hill in a matter of minutes for an affordable 10 euro fee.

- **Luza Square, Dubrovnik**-One of the busiest squares in Croatia, Luza Square is also the location of historic landmark Sponza Place, the city's famous bell tower, and St. Blaise's Church. During the warmer months, they host the Dubrovnik Summer Festival, which features live music, local food, and plenty of activities to do for children of all ages.

- **Browse the Markets** - All of Croatia's Markets do not charge a fee to browse the artisanal goods. Check out our Shopping chapter for the best places to go!

- **National Parks**-The National Parks offer amazing views and is free of charge. Whether you're looking to hike, photograph the sites, or relax in a remote area, the National Parks are beautiful and unique. North Velebit National Park, Paklenica National Park, Kornati National Park, Krka National Park, Risnjak National Park, or Plitvice Lakes National Park are all great options with breathtaking sites.

ENJOY THE HOTEL BREAKFAST AND FIND THE SUPERMARKETS

If you're balling on a budget, spending money three times a day for meals and snacks can add up. Most hotels in Croatia offer a continental breakfast, and by taking advantage of this complimentary service, you'll end up cutting corners. For lunch, choose one of the many street lined cafes or outdoor markets. From grabbing a cup of coffee to enjoying a local delicacy such as Pršut, we recommend you spend your lunch exploring. The busier cities such as Zagreb offer many restaurants and café options. The choices are often reasonably priced and have a large variety to choose from. If heading on an "off the beaten path" adventure, make sure to pack a lunch!

ASK A LOCAL! FIND COUPONS AND DISCOUNTS

If staying in a hotel, the concierge can offer restaurant and activity discounts. If staying with locals, ask them on their favorite spots. No one knows better than someone who lives there! Make sure to take advantage!

CHAPTER 7:
CRASH GUIDE TO CROATIA'S BEST SHOPPING STORES

For those with a passion for fashion and decadent dishes, Croatia offers you plenty of both!

Shoo-and-hop is the name of the game in Croatia's island landscape. If you're looking for a bargain, top designer brands, or indigenous souvenirs, you'll be sure to find exactly what you're looking for at these top locations.

TRAVEL ESSENTIALS

Make sure to wear comfortable shoes as you shop until you drop! Sandals or heels can be tricky when walking on some of the cobbled roads. As we've said before, take advantage of local transportation and hop on and off a bus! The bus has stops along the way, so you won't get lost trying to find transportation.

ESSENTIAL EXPERIENCES

- Get lunch at the Outdoor Market in Trznica/Pazar
- Appreciate the local artistry at Plitvicka Iezera National Park
- Keep your credit card at bay…or don't at the marble-lined street of Marmontova
- Don't forget your sunglasses! For sunnier weather or to help your market "bidding poker face".

OUTDOOR MARKET, TRZNICA / PAZAR –

On eastern side of the Diocletian Palace, you'll find everything that you were looking for and oodles more. This is a location that will make you wish you'd packed an extra suitcase, and with how much you can save, you can afford to buy one and pay check it on your flight. You'll find clothing and accessory bargains from Croatia and China, affordable and top-of-the-line goods from Turkey, and playful souvenirs from surrounding islands like Livno or island of Pag. You'll also find vegetables, fruits and flowers, all from local farms near Split. Don't forget to bargain your prices – they take a nosedive in the afternoon/evenings!

Malls, Zagreb

Capitol Center is relatively new mall, opening just over a decade ago in Zagreb. Its prime location is just a 10-minute walk from Main Square and near a sports arena. Just southwest of the city center, the mall is situated next to a sports arena. It's a great place to dodge a rainy day, offering an IMAX theatre, bowling alley, food court, and over 200 stores. There's also plenty of parking for tourists with care rentals and natives alike.

Hrelic, Zagreb

Known as Croatia's largest and most diverse flea market, Hrelic is the place to get unique souvenirs and antiques. The name of the game is bargaining, so be sure to bring cash currency and wear your poker face to get the best deals. Important travel tip: the flea market does not offer shade opportunities, so be sure to bring a hat, sunscreen, and sunglasses if traveling to Hrelic in the summer.

LOCAL CRAFTS & SOUVENIRS, PLITVICKA JEZERA NATIONAL PARK

The souvenir shop you've been looking for! Located at the National Park, you'll be able to find your standard t-shirts, key chains, etc., with beautiful images of the stunning Croatian landscape. In addition to a host of your usual souvenirs, you'll also find unique artwork, crafted trinkets, and even handcrafted dolls. It's fair prices and beautiful location makes it a perfect shop stop.

MARMONTOVA ULICA STREET, SPLIT

The marble-lined street of Marmontova is paradise for designer shopping fanatics. While sifting through designer deals, you'll also take in the beautiful locations, which runs from the waterfront all the way back to the Trg Gaje Bulata, which is where the Croatian National Theatre is located.

You'll find your favorite jewelry, clothing, shoes and other goods from household brands such as Versace, Armani, and Dolce & Gabana. Sprinkled in the shopping are a few restaurants and unique, specialized shops to break up the experience, too.

Hrvatsko Zagorje

North of Zagreb lies an area of Croatia that takes pride in its homemade crafts and artisanal work. They've been making toys by hand there for ages, applying simple skills that never died out.

Best places to see these crafty toymakers in action are Marija Bistrica and surrounding villages. Other Croatian cultural traditions are two-part folk singing in the coastal regions, and lacemaking in Pag, Lepoglava and Hvar.

WHAT TO BUY IN CROATIA:

Handcraft Goods: Croatia is known for their locally made ceramics and carvings. However these items are time consuming to make and ornate, but they are not budget friendly.

Neckties: It is believed that neckties were originally invented in Croatia, although nearby Italy has probably influenced their style a bit more with fashion sense.

Slivovic: Very strong local plum schnapps. The liquor is extremely sweet and can be sipped after dinner.

CHAPTER 8:
CROATIAN BEACHES YOU MUST ABSOLUTELY GO TO

What's island hopping without comparing the best beaches? Most are content with the formulaic sand, sun, water routine, and who can blame them. But, Croatia's unique topography adds layers of personality to their beaches, with each island giving you more to explore and their own signature experiences. These breathtaking characters of these top beaches are the perfect way to round out your trip.

Bačvice, Split – This city beach is a haven not just for tourists, but for locals as well. Natives to this part of split view the beach as an integral part of their development, as an outlet for social, athletic, and even spiritual experiences. It's home to the game picigin, a ball game played in the water. The aqua water is warm and shallow, which allows you to delve deep into the water and immerse yourself in the incredible 360 view, which includes greenery, mountains, peeks into the city, and of course the bustling beach. Because it's such a city stronghold, the beach is buzzing with friendly people, food, and nightlife. It's also one of the few sandy beaches that Croatia has to offer.

Kraljičina plaza, NIN – This exotic location offers you a blend of a traditional beach experience with quirks of Croatian culture. A long strip of sandy beaches outside Zadar, Nin's long, luxuriant Kraljičina plaža is a true experience, disturbed only by a few bars and not too much little else. The brilliant blue water is accompanied by the Velebit Mountains across the way. No wonder it translates to Queen's Beach! You may be distracted by locals bathing themselves is a sludgy, muddy substance near the reeds behind Kraljičina plaza. It's actually an earth bearing treatment for sore muscles and joints, rich in peloids, which aid in this relief.

Spiaza, Susak – If you came to Croatia to get away, this is the beach for you. While many of the beaches are accessible in an effort to boost tourism, the desert island getaway is a ferry ride away from the already distant Mali Lošinj. The ride is a beautiful one, and its isolation unlocks extra appeal for the true beach connoisseur appeal. Susak village's main beach is Spiaza, a shallow bay that forces you half a kilometer out before it's deep enough to swim. You'll feel the any stresses you have melt away with each step further into the water – and further away from reality! To escape even further, challenge yourself to walk the rocky heartland and discover other beaches and private alcoves.

Kupari – Looking for an adventure like no other? The Kupari beach experience isn't cut out of a brochure, but it's an experience all of Croatia's own. Kupari is located just south of Dubrovnik, and was once one of the finest vacation destinations for Yugoslav Peoples' Army. After weathering war damages from 1991–95 war, it is now largely abandoned, with isolated, shell-damaged hotels giving it an apocalyptic feel. The beach, however, remains stunning, and one of the Dubrovnik region's finest, with a half moon stretch of sand and turquoise waters. While the post-apocalyptic feel isn't exactly the stereotypical beach dream, it does capture a part of the country's history and yield an entirely unique experience. Note that exploring is potentially dangerous, as the abandoned hotels are not protected.

THE ESSENTIAL BEACH PACKING LIST

The sun's out, the water is glistening in the distance, and you can't wait to go outside and catch some rays. However, when you're on vacation, it's easy to forget the essentials when packing. Although many beach souvenir and pharmacies may offer travel size versions of anything you need, many shops tend to take advantage of the accidental memory slip and inflate the prices. Here's our list of vital beach essentials to help you be prepared and save money.

Water-Hydrate. Hydrate. Hydrate. Doctors recommend the average person should drink 8 full glasses a day. When you're in the sun, you should drink even more to take into account the heat and your body working overtime to keep you cool. If you can't bring bottles of water, at least bring a water bottle in your suitcase to save you money.

Bathing Suit-In all the excitement of your travel, forgetting your bathing suit is a large possibility. Make sure to put it at the top of your packing list!

Sunscreen-The Mediterranean breeze may feel cooler and the sun may feel less harsh, but the sunburn at night when you're trying to turn over to sleep wont'! Make sure to test out a few different grades of SPF so that you know which one works for your skin.

Extra Blanket-We highly recommend bringing an extra blanket for any journey. An extra blanket can come in handy for a variety of instances. If you're on the train or plane and the air conditioning is on high or the heat isn't cutting it, an extra blanket can keep you cozy. Same goes for when you're staying in your hotel room! In this instance, an extra blanket can be used as something to lay or sit on at the beach. Blankets are heavier than towels, and will be easier to keep on the ground instead of blowing away.

Flip Flops-Flip Flops should be a vital travel essential when going away. They're easy to slide on and off your feet, so your feet won't have to battle trying to get into a close toed shoe when its covered in sand and wet. They're lightweight, so they won't weigh down your suitcase, and help ease the pain of hot sand on your feet. Additionally, flip flops are great to have for those staying in accommodations when you're sharing a shower with other guests.

Water Shoes-Many of the beaches in Croatia are rocky. If you're heading to explore one of these beaches, water shoes may be your new best friend. By bringing shoes that protect the bottoms of your feet and drain quickly, you can go from water to beach at ease.

Sunglasses-It may seem like a silly thing to put on the list, as sunglasses should be brought all the time, but you'd be surprised when packing all the things you need to for a long journey and they go forgotten. Sunglasses protect your eyes, and you'll look great in all those selfies you'll be taking.

Change of Clothes-Who wants to walk around in wet clothes back to the hotel? Make sure to bring an extra pair of clothes so that you can easy transition from the beach to grab something to eat or walk around town!

First Aid Kit-It doesn't have to be large or bulky, but again you should have this for any vacation. By bringing a few essentials such as band aids, ibuprofen, cold medication, and antibiotic ointment, you'll be prepared for any scenario!

CHAPTER 9:
WHERE TO DINE AND WHAT TO EAT IN CROATIA

CROATIA'S LOCAL DELICACIES

Trying indigenous foods when you're traveling can unlock windows – and flavors – into culture that you've never previously had access to. Exposing yourself to new and delicious food is a great way to bond with locals, learn about where in the country the food is from, how it's made, and the history.

It's little wonder that sharing food and drink plays such a big part in the culture in Croatia, when the country is blessed with such top-notch ingredients from both the sea and land. Simple home-style cooking is the main feature of family-run taverns, but increasingly a new breed of chefs are bringing a more "farm to table" and adventurous approach to dining. Meanwhile local delicacies like Croatian wines and olive oils are making their mark on the world stage, garnering top awards and becoming more and more internationally recognized. Though Croats traditionally see themselves as a Western country with its close proximity to Italy, many of the food staples in Croatia resemble Balkan culture.

Our list of top indigenous Croatian foods is sure to give you something for any taste to try in your travels.

Pršut – This specialty dry-cured ham is on virtually every menu and a part of every Croatian celebration. In order to be prepared properly, it has to undergo Croatia's fall/winter season. The cold, salty Adriatic wind is what gives it such unique taste and texture. It's served in long, skinny slices (the cutting of which is an art form) with cheese and/or olives. It can be served as a full entrée or as a snack.

Pašticada – This is a traditional Dalmatian beef dish. The most important part is in the preparation more than the cooking, as it marinates for at least 24 hours in red wine. It's also soaked in rosemary and sage, garlic and other herbs. Plums, onions, cloves, nutmeg, and carrots are added during the cooking process for additional flavor, creating a think, dark sauce.

Brudet – On the lighter side of these meat heavy indigenous dishes is a fish stew from Istria and parts of Dalmatia. It's made with not one but with several types of fish, and bathed in tomato sauce in a single pot. The most unique part of this recipe is that the pot is meant to be shaken, not stirred, clearly a James Bond inspiration. Prepping at a low temperature allows the juices of the fish to intensify the flavor.

Tartufi – While vegetables aren't traditionally Croatia's signature food, the Istria region gives us these powerful mushrooms believed to be an aphrodisiac. A unique food, they grow underground, and specially trained dogs are the ones who locate them. Their powerful flavor and fragrance may not line up with their appearance, but they pack a lot of punch when enhancing a meal.

Ispod peke – This isn't a stand-alone food per say, but actually a method of cooking. If your food is being prepped with this method, you're in for a delicious surprise. Typically, the cook puts a meat ingredient like lamb or veal paired with potatoes into a stone oven under a metal cover. Then he/she covers the cover in hot coals and lets it be. The food cooks slowly and requires no additional attention, just marinating in it's own juices. The coals intensify the flavor, creating a delicious, colorful meal.

CROATIA'S BEST RESTAURANTS

One of the most exciting staples to explore about another culture is its food. With such a unique geographical personality, Croatia celebrates its culture through some edible common threads, but each island also has their own specialties. Here are some of our favorite restaurants in Croatia:

Konoba Kala, Brac Island – Konoba Kala is one of the most well known food establishments in Povlja. It's delicious food, waterside location, and amazing customer service offer a winning combination. It's pristine reputation draws in tourists, and it's consistency draws in locals, gathering a mix of patrons that are social and well fed! For an optimal experience, plan on a sunset dinner, preferably with one of their flavorful seafood options.

Boskinac, Island of Pag – Whether it's a couple's getaway or a family friendly vibe, Boskinac has something for everyone. This hotel and restaurant offers a relaxed atmosphere, and sits upon one of the few plush green lawns in the city. It's outdoor escape, delicious menu, and decor are an expression of the Croatian culture. The friendly wait staff knows not only their menu, but also plenty about the significance of the artwork inside and the intricacies of the land on which they sit. While they do a great job of offering tasty twists on standard meals, they also boast a brag-worthy wine selection. Don't believe us? They've been featured on food and culture extraordinaire Anthony Bourdain's show.

Boca Vera, Mali Losinj – How can you travel somewhere without knowing where to pick up the best slice of pizza? That's just one of the many delicious dishses at Boca Vera. Ranging from incredible seafood to the best pizza in town, their diverse menu caters to everyone in your travel party. While resort dining can sometimes lead to a mediocre experience, this will give you just the opposite with a beautiful view, fair prices, and an English-speaking wait staff that can provide you with perfect recommendations. Heads up – they don't take credit cards!

Adriatic Sushi & Oyster, Split – If you're going to dine by the sea, you've got to indulge. Adriatic Sushi & Oyster bar will make sure there are no regrets about doing so, providing you with outstanding seafood that's sure to have you asking for seconds. Whether you're a sushi starter or a seafood pro, their menu and skilled wait staff will cater to the experience that you desire. The atmosphere is relaxed but stunning, located in the Diocletian palace and offering indoor and outdoor seating.

The Garden, Zadar – For the ultimate outdoor relaxation dining experience, The Garden is top notch in Zadar. Whether you're looking for a full meal or a few cocktails, The Garden offers you lounger beds, outdoor curtain, and fresh air overlooking the sea. Its accompanied by great music and a friendly wait staff. The balance between a cozy atmosphere and open space makes it the perfect date night or adult hang.

TIPS WHEN DINING ABROAD

With many mobile apps out there today to tell you where to go and what to eat, many don't exactly say what to wear or how to act. The idea of dining out seems extremely straightforward and simple to find a restaurant, eat, and leave. However, when you add foreign-language menus, servers who might not speak your language, and unfamiliar cultural quirks, the experience often prove to be a bit more difficult than you anticipated.

Each country has its own customs and routines that may seem forward or off.

Here are our tips for navigating through the twists and turns of local restaurant customs and making the dining experience one to remember...in a good way!

Do Your Research About the Dress Code Ahead of Time-The last thing you want to do is show up to a fancy restaurant in your wet beach attire. Do a little research online or ask the hotel staff beforehand if they could call or are aware of the dress code. Some stricter restaurants also expect men to wear long pants or women to have their shoulders covered. It's worth taking the few minutes to check instead of being turned away at the door.

Use Simple Language or Gestures-Although a language barrier can be frustrating, busier tourist cities often have servers who may be able to speak English or understand common phrases. When all else fails, point or gesture to try to explain. You'll be surprised how easy it is to communicate.

Learn the Lingo-Imagine how nicer it is to ask for a bill in the language of your server instead of making grand gestures and yelling "bill!" over and over? By knowing a few words or phrases you'll help your situation, rather than harm it!

Know when to tip - Countries like Japan and China have fees in the meal to account for tip. Do tip in America. Many countries in Europe incorporate tipping into the meal prices or where a service charge is automatically included, but you can round the bill up if you want to leave extra for your waiter. Do your research so you're not paying more!

Relax- You're on vacation! Stress should be far from your mind. You're not the first tourist who has ever stopped into their restaurant, so don't become stressed or embarrassed for the language barrier. Go with the flow and understand the staff is there to help you. It may seem frustrating, but the more impatient or upset you show, the less willing they will be to help you. Communication goes both ways!

<u>How to use the Destination Chapter Listings</u>

Each listing in the guide is designed to be concise and easy to follow.

The travel essentials section is for orientating yourself in the area.

Essential experiences are the popular, well-known, and well-visited attractions in an area.

Noteworthy hidden gems are listed in the destination guide

The names of attractions and experiences are highlighted in bold.

Addresses and websites are provided in the entry

The best culinary experiences are detailed in the where to eat section. This guide strives to only present good value and good food options. Indicative prices are shown on a scale of $ (cheap) to $$$ (very expensive).

Where to drink and party details the kind of vibe to expect in the area, from raucous all night partying to sipping coffee on elegant terraces. The individual listings highlight a few of the best options.

Insider's tip offers a real insight from a local living in the area.

****

CHAPTER 10: ZAGREB

TRAVEL ESSENTIALS:

Zagreb is Croatia's largest city as well as the country's capital. Due to many wanting to spend their time perusing the costal beaches and picturesque waters, Zagreb is often overlooked by tourists. However, do not over look this city! Zagreb offers plenty to do with its diverse list of museums, galleries, restaurants, cafes, and extensive nightlife.

The city is split into three parts: the thousand-year old Gornji grad (known today as Upper Town) which contains the Presidential Palace, the iconic St Mark's Church, the Croatian parliament (Sabor), and plenty of museums and galleries that give Zagreb its nickname as the "city of museums". Bask in the romantic views of cobbled streets at night which are lit by gas lamps; the 19th century Donji grad (Lower Town) with its shops, restaurants, cafes, theatres and parks; and the modern post-World War II area of Novi Zagreb ("new Zagreb") which offers modern architecture such as full of high-rise corporate buildings. For delicious Austrian Balkan infused restaurants, downtown is the place to be. Lower Town was designed during the Austro-Hungarian monarchy and it's the reason why Zagreb is called " small Vienna".

Zagreb is an easy commuter city, as everything is a light walk from all the transportation (tram and bus) stops. The average trip costs just 4 kunas (approx 0.80 cents) and stops allow you to travel up to the Upper Town, or also know as the historic district. As we've said before, Zagreb is an easy commuter city, so feel free to skip the transportation and walk up to the Upper Town on a brisk 15-20 minute walk. Along the way be sure to stop at the local artisan shops and bakeries! The Upper Town has one of the best views in the city of Zagreb from below.

We recommend visiting the complex of Cathedral of The Assumption of Virgin Mary and the Archbishop's palace. Make sure to add time to wander aimlessly like a Croat through Dolac Market and enjoy a coffee on the famous Tkalčićeva street. For the history buffs, head to the Upper Town where to view a Parliament building, Croatian government and Old City Hal.

ESSENTIAL EXPERIENCES:

- **The Museum of Broken Relationships**-This museum is unique because it doesn't cater or tell the story of anyone famous, but more so of those who are looking for closure in life that they may have never received. Individuals from around the world donate items that remind them of lost love along with the story that explains the item's significance. https://brokenships.com

- **St. Mark's Church**-St. Mark's Church is one of the most famous historical sites in all of Croatia, not to mention the city. The Croatians love to show off pride for their country, and they do so on the roof of St. Mark's. The tiled roof features the coat of arms of Croatia, Dalmatia and Slavonia

- **Trg Bana Jelacica/Ban Jelacic Square**- This is the main square in Zagreb and offers historical sites and dining options. Look for the iconic Mandusevac Fountain and take a picture! Or, head to one of the cafes and people watch while drinking coffee (or wine).

- **Zagreb Cathedral**-This neo-Gothic styled Church offers remnants of the original Cathedral that once stood there dating back to the 13th century. After an earthquake in the late 1800s, the Cathedral was rebuilt with twin neo-gothic spires. It's walking distance to Dolac market.

- **Dolac Market**-Zagreb's largest market that offers local food, homemade crafts, and artisanal favorites.

- **Jarun Lake**- Instead of heading to the ocean, Jarun Lake offers its own sandy beaches that are perfect for swimming and sunbathing. For the adventurous, Jarun Lake also offers reserved areas are specifically for wind-surfers, pedalo boats and canoes. For a less crowded option, Bundek Lake also offers free swimming during the summer months, along with free live music performances held on its summer performance stage.

- **Walk through classic Zagreb**

- **Greta Centrally** located and constantly transitioning, Gallery Greta is one of the more popular attractions in Zagreb. A new exhibition opens every Monday

WHERE TO EAT:

- **Palainovka**-Known by the locals (although unconfirmed) to be the oldest cafe in Zagreb (dating back to1846), this Viennese-style place serves delicious coffee, tea and cakes under pretty ornate ceilings. The café is open late nights so whether you need an early breakfast or a post nightlife treat, Palainovka should be high on your list.

- **Vinodol**- The Central European style restaurant is a local and tourist favorite, and its easy to see why. Whether dining in the dining hall or under the romantic ivy covered patio, the comfort food options such as veal and potatoes www.vinodol-zg.hr will ensure a full belly and sound sleep

- **Kaptolska** Klet-A beer hall, live music, and a terrace? Sign us up! This Eastern European restaurant offers local Zagreb specialties, including homemade breads and sausages.

- **Karijola**-The thin crust Mediterranean style pizzeria is a local and tourist favorite. Using local Croatian ingredients, the pizza is baked in a clay oven to crispy perfection. We like to think that the thinner the crust on the pizza…the more you can eat!

- **Didov San**-Head to Zagreb's Upper Town to dine with the locals and enjoy this rustic tavern style restaurant. We recommend you call ahead and make reservations, as the smaller restaurant tends to fill up quickly. www.konoba-didovsan.com

WHERE TO DRINK AND EXPERIENCE NIGHTLIFE:

- **Kino Europa**- Dating back to the 1920's, Kino Europa is Zagreb's oldest cinema. Today, it's been renovated to become a noteworthy cafe, wine bar and grapperia . This glass-enclosed space also offers an exquisite outdoor terrace where you can enjoy coffee, over 30 types of grappa and the comfortable amenities of free wi-fi. The cinema hosts film screenings and occasional dance parties on the weekends. www.kinoeuropa.hr

- **Cica**-For that are looking to party like a local, Cica is the place to be. This tiny bar is hidden behind a storefront and is almost invisible to the untrained eye on Tkalčićeva. The funky interior has modern work by local artists and cool flea market finds. Sample one all of the 25 kinds of rakija (a fruit brandy popular in the Balkans) that the place is famous for. Looking for sweet? Sour? Fruity? Nutty? Think about your wildest dream flavor, and Cica has it.

CHAPTER 11:
DUBROVNIK & SOUTHERN DALMATIA

TRAVEL ESSENTIALS:

Dubrovnik is one of the most beautiful and diverse cities in Croatia. It's not surprising that its airport attracts the second highest number of tourists per year. No matter the time of the year, it's easy to see thousands of visitors strolling along the gorgeous marble streets and staring at the high medieval walls, in awe of the cities' beauty. The city not only offers a lot in itself, but it is also a great starting point for your travel journey. To the northwest lies the island of Korčula where rural plains sprawl across the island for a beautiful natural untouched habitat. To the southeast of Dubrovnik lies the adventurous island of Konayle, which is a local and tourist favorite for beach seekers, wine lovers and history fanatics.

Fun Fact: The popular international television show Game of Thrones has been filmed numerous times in Dubrovnik!

EXPERIENCE ESSENTIALS:

- **Mljet Island**- The majority of the island is covered by small villages, wineries, and untouched forests. If looking to go off the beaten path and hike or get in touch with nature, Mljet National Park offers scenic forests and tranquil saltwater lakes. Mljet was mentioned in the tale of Odysseus, who remained on Mljet Island for seven years basking in its serene oasis.

- **Trsteno Gardens**- These 16th century gardens has both medieval and renaissance design inspirations. Gorgeous Mediterranean plants like lavender, citrus orchids, and water lilies add color to every nook of the sprawling grounds. There's a maze the children can walk through, and a large pond that makes you feel inspired to paint like Monet.

- **Cable Cars**-Take a cable car north of Dubrovnik high to Mt. Srd in a matter of minutes. View the breathtaking views of Dubrovnik from above for some unforgettable photos.

- **St. Mark's Cathedral**-This revered Renaissance Italian styled church is one of the most noteworthy cathedrals in Croatia. The 15th century ornate details are stunning. Beware of long lines in the summer seasons.

- **Pile Gate**-In 1537, the city gate was built for protection to the city. A statue of St. Blaise stands overlooking anyone who enters the gate and into the city.

- **Onoforio Fountain**- The Onofrio Fountain was built in 1438 as part of a water-supply system. It is one of the most noted landmarks in Dubrovnik.

- **Banje Beach**-This rocky beach is popular for both tourists and locals. Its location is right outside Old Town. Bring your bathing suits and water shoes to avoid cutting up your feet. Umbrellas and chairs are available for rent on site.

- **Uje**-For those looking to bring back something special for loved ones back home, stop in to Uje. They specialize in selling the best local made olive oils, jams, and spices that's perfect for any gift.

- **Luza Square, Dubrovnik**-One of the busiest squares in Croatia, Luza Square is also the location of historic landmark Sponza Place, the city's famous bell tower, and St. Blaise's Church. During the warmer months, they host the Dubrovnik Summer Festival, which features live music, local food, and plenty of activities to do for children of all ages.

- Walk the cobbled streets to view the fortress walls and view the medieval architecture

WHERE TO EAT:

- **Nautika Restaurant**-Chef Mario Bunda creates a customized menu for you at the top restaurant in Dubrovnik, with extraordinary and complex dishes while offering an incredible view of Old Town and the sea while you dine.

- **Restaurant 360**-If you appreciate fine culinary dishes, Restaurant 360 will be sure to "wow" you. Known as Dubrovnik's most exclusive fine dining establishments, the dishes offer unique flavors, classic dishes with a twist, and local ingredients incorporated for an homage to all things Croat.

- **Bugenvilla**-One of the trendiest restaurants on Cavtat's seafront, this European infused restaurant has brightly colored décor and unique dishes to make the overall dining experience fun.

- **Oyster & Sushi Bar Bota Šare**-You can't travel to the seashore without getting seafood! The Oyster & Sushi bar offers fresh and local seafood, as well as options to sit on the terrace and overlook views of Dubrovnik

- **Cukarin**-If you're looking for a "grab and go" option, this deli is simple and to the point. Offering homemade breads, pastries, and bites, we recommend grabbing something for the beach and enjoying a picnic later on.

WHERE TO DRINK AND PARTY:

- **Cave Bar More**-Both a local and tourist favorite, this beach bar may be small in size, but packs a lot of fun into its space. Whether you're looking for a nightcap, cocktail, after dinner coffee, or post dancing snack, Cave Bar More has it all. It's relaxing atmosphere isn't what makes this top our list. The actual bar is set in a cave and the glass floor peers down onto a water filled cavern. Only in Croatia. www.hotel-more.hr

- **Lazareti**-Any local or tour guide will tell you to head to Lazareti for the experience. Although busier on the tourist perspective, Lazareti offers a lot of fun in one central area. Offering movie nights, club nights, and live music, Lazareti packs in a lot of culture. www.lazareti.com

- **Cocktail Bar Massimo**-Accessible only by ladder (trust us!), this bar is located in Zakerjan Tower and worth the trek for the experience. The drinks are brought up in pulleys. Visit for the views and the experience. It's definitely picture worthy!

- **Gaffe**-If you're looking to live like a local, Gaffe is your bar. The Croatian owned Irish pub is filled with screaming Croats when football is on. If it's not, check out the covered terrace of this comfortable pub.

- **Club Revelin**- A renovated 16th-century fortress that marks the eastern end of Old Town has become the "go to" trendy bar. Who doesn't want to say they've drank in a fortress?

- **East-West Club**-By night it's a trendy club and beach bar, but by day it's a restaurant filled with delicious dishes. Go ahead and have a cocktail on the beach.

CHAPTER 12: ISTRIA

TRAVEL ESSENTIALS:

Istria is known for its extensive wine and cuisine culture. The peninsula that Istria lies on is the largest in the Adriatic Sea. Because of it's close proximity to Italy, many locals speak Italian. Wines such as moscato, trebbiano and verduzzo can be found flourishing in Istria's hillside vineyards. Terrano, a varietal with denominazione di origine controllata ("controlled designation of origin") protection in Italy's Friuli-Venezia Giulia region, is grown here, on the western edge of peninsula, in red clay soil that can be compared to that of northern Italy's terra rossa ("red earth").

Besides it's extensive wine country, in Istria you'll find medieval towns on the hillside, as well towns that may confuse your coordinates and make you think that you are in Italy. The region is known for having some of the best olive oil and white truffle grown locally. Cyclists are found up and down the hillside, as the locals stay extremely active and the tourists come to bicycle along the breathtaking views up and down the rolling hills.

If you're traveling with children, Istria offers a water park called Aquapark, which is fun for all ages.

Istria is also close to a lot of other islands and cities to explore. The island-scattered Kvarner Gulf, located south of Istria, is presided over by the city of Rijeka, a busy commerce and port city with an energetic cultural life. Not far offshore on the Kvarner Gulf, the Kvarner islands of Cres, Lošinj and Krkhave offers both luxurious beach resorts and retained its fair share of quiet seaside villages and tranquil coves.

EXPERIENCE ESSENTIALS:

- Bike miles upon miles viewing lush vineyards in the wine country. Stop into the little town of Novigrad, a quaint little town located on a peninsula in Istria that is overflowing with cafes, brightly colored houses, a harbor with local seafood, and of course wine.

- **Euphrasian Basilica**- This 6th-century Euphrasian Basilica is one of Europe's finest intact examples of Byzantine art. Built originally on the site of a 4th-century oratory, the sacral complex consists of a religious church, an atrium and a baptistery. Tourists can take in the breathtaking glittering wall of ornate mosaics in the apse. These 6th-century masterpieces feature biblical scenes, archangels and Istrian martyrs.

- **Roman Amphitheater**-Pula's most famous tourist attraction, this Roman Empire era amphitheater was once built to hold gladiators. Today, it still draws in a crowd as an architecture wonder and a venue for concerts and plays in the summer.

- **Pazin's Kaštel**- Feel like you've stepped back into the Medieval times as Pazin's Kaštel is the largest and best-preserved medieval structure in Istria. Its architecture has hints of design inspiration from Romanesque, Gothic and Renaissance architecture. Historians believe the structure was built somewhere around 1000 A.D. Today, Pazin's Kašte has two museums inside; one that contains an exhibition about slave revolts, and torture instruments in the dungeon. The other museum has rougly 4200 artifacts portraying traditional Istrian village life, including garments, tools and pottery.

- **Fonticus Gallery**-Appreciate local and national artists at the Fonticus Gallery. The gallery focuses solely on Croatian artists, as well as celebrates Croatia's independence with a small exhibit on war helmets and weapons throughout the centuries.

- Go on a wine tour. Due to the region's similarities to Italy, Istria's wine culture is similar to Italy. Check out Kozlovic Winery, Kabola Winery, Cuj Winery, Trapan Winery, or Roxanich Winery for some of the best wines in Croatia.

- Visit the hilltop towns of Motovun and Groznjan

WHERE TO EAT:

Konoba Batelina-If you're looking for fine seafood dishes, look no more. This family-run tavern is located just outside Pula, Istria. The restaurant chef and owner is also the fisherman for the restaurant, and proudly serves his prized catch of the day. The restaurant is warm, eclectic, and delicious. Make sure to book a reservation ahead.

Agroturizam Nežić-For those looking to have a true Mediterranean meal, the restaurant Agroturizam Nežić offers light and homemade dishes in the "farm to table" mindset. Owners Nadia and Paolo make everything from the most natural ingredients. From fresh crusty bread served with homemade olive oil, to antipasto salads and fresh cheeses, you won't find a more traditional Mediterranean meal than the one here. The tavern is small and fills up quick so make sure to make a reservation, or be prepared to wait.

Maestral-This tavern located on the seaside of Rovinj is as romantic as it gets. The tables over amazing views of the old town along the sea edge. It's still under the tourist radar, so you'll find more locals enjoying the cuisine than tourists. You're welcome.

The Wine Vault-This French-Mediterranean styled restaurant is located inside the Hotel Monte Mulini. It offers "farm to table" dishes, all based on a variety of seasonal ingredients.

WHERE TO DRINK AND EXPERIENCE NIGHTLIFE:

- **Cabahia**-This artsy garden terrace located in Pula is always busy with locals and tourists. During warmer months, it hosts concerts on the weekends, and can become crowed. Make sure to get there early and bring a blanket if you want to sit outside in the grass.
- **Saint & Sinner**-This trendy bar is captures all modern European

charm. Decorated in only black and white, be prepared to dress up and drink up with the locals on this waterfront "place to be".

- **Aruba**-This bar and club turns from a relaxing beachy vibe bar to a trendy dance club as soon as the sun sets. The outdoor terrace is usually packed and the music inside will keep your feet moving.

- **Zanzibar**-As luxurious as the name sounds; Zanzibar is an upscale cocktail bar for the mixology fans. Dark Indonesian wood brings a sexy vibe to this bar that has remnants of both tropical and romance in the scenery.

- **Punta Corrente Forest Park**-Established in the late 19th century, the park allows you to cycle or walk through. Be sure to bring your bathing suit and go for a swim off the shore, or at least a blanket to stop and watch the sunset fade over the water.

CHAPTER 13: SPLIT

TRAVEL ESSENTIALS:

Split is known as Dalmatia's sassiest city. Its city is set surrounding by dramatic coastal mountains that act as the perfect backdrop to the Adriatic Sea's gorgeous turquoise waters. Split is the second largest city in Croatia. Besides the historical landmark Diocletian's Palace, its nightlife and restaurant culture is thriving. The city is seen as a central hub, as it's the main gateway to many of the islands. In the summer months, Split is known for its festivals such as Olympic Sailing Week or the Croatia Boat Show. Split also celebrates the Days of Marulic Croatian Theatre Festival and the Split Marathon in April; the feast of Saint Domnius in May; and the Mediterranean Film Festival and Croatia Reggae Festival in June.

EXPERIENCE ESSENTIALS:

- **Diocletian's Palace**: Originally built in the Roman Period, and built upon in the Middle Ages, Diocletian's Palace has been used as a military fortress, imperial residence and fortified town. Traveler Tip: Each Gate is named after a metal Bronze, Gold, Silver, and Iron)

- **Island hop on a cruise to Hvar Island from Split**. Split's coastal port is a popular starting point for island cruises and offers a variety of boat choices. From boats, cruise ships, ferries, and catamarans; you can choose whatever boat you would like based on time, destination, and budget.

- **Croatian National Theater-**The theater offers opera, ballet, theater, and music performances.

- **Bastijana Winery**-One of the oldest wineries in Europe, the winery that's been making wine for more than 2,000 years.
- Take a walking tour through **Diocletian's** palace, the old town, produce markets, fish markets, and Marjan Park
- **Archeological Museum, Split**-Located next to the National Theater, the Archeological Museum offers key historical discoveries that unlock our history's past. Release your inner history buff and view relics of past civilizations such as mosaics and paintings.

WHERE TO EAT:

- **Figa**- This quaint restaurant has a fun atmosphere, delicious food, and live music. Need we say more?
- **Luxor**-Luxor gives you the chance to people watch the locals and enjoy coffee and cake in the cathedral. Cushions are sprawled along the cathedral's steps for a relaxed vibe.
- **Libar**-The portions are large, the breakfasts are noteworthy, and they have tapas and a big screen to watch sports games with the locals. It's a quiet restaurant that takes you away from the tourist buzz.

WHERE TO DRINK AND DANCE:

- **Imperium**-Splits only "superclub" is the place to go if you're looking to dance the night away. Imperium offers two dance floors, and an outdoor bar. It's usually busy on the weekends so expect crowds.
- **Ghetto**-This fun and gay friendly bar is trendy, relaxed and a great spot to hang out with the locals for a low-key drink.

CHAPTER 14: EXPLORING SOME OF CROATIA'S BEST ISLANDS

HVAR: CROATIA'S LITTLE IBIZA

Hvar is the quintessential ideals of a Croatian island It's the most luxurious island, and one of the sunniest places in the country for sunbathing and being outdoors. Hvar is also known for its lavender fields, as well as other aromatic herbs such as rosemary and heather. Travelers wander along the main square (St. Stephen's Square) of Hvar Town, explore the sights on the winding cobbled stone streets, Hvar Cathedral, Spanish fortress, the Arsenal and the Theatre. When heading to the island, make sure to swim on the numerous beaches or take a boat or water taki to the nudist beaches on the Pakleni Islands or take a walk to the southern cliffs for a lunch at the local winery.

If looking to dance the night away and have some cocktails, check out Carpe Diem, Kiva Bar, and Nautica. Stari Grad and Jelsa, Hvar's other two towns that offer quieter, charming options with less inflated prices.

Cres: Best Adventure Island

Cres is an untouched and wild island for those looking to be away from civilization and appreciate natural beauty. It's ideal for the adventurer looking to forge their own path around overgrown forests, get in touch with nature, swim in reclusive coves and sampling some of Croatia's traditional delicacy: lamb. Cres' natural freshwater lake of Vrana is actually one of the deepest freshwater lakes in Eastern Europe. Watersports, scuba diving, and hiking are all popular activities on Cres.

Brač: Best Beach Island

Brač is the largest Adriatic island. The island also has Croatia's most famous and popular beach: Zlatni Rat near Bol. Tourists and locals head to Zlatni Rat for light water sports, windsurfing, paddleboarding, swimming, kite surfing, and and sunbathing. Vidova Gora Mountain, the tallest mountain in the area, and is also definitely worth a visit. If you're adventurous side is getting the best of you, think about visiting the numerous private coves and pebble beaches on Brač. Dragon Cave is a popular attraction as well.

Mljet (South Dalmatia): Best Island to Get in Touch with Nature

The majority of the island is covered by small villages, wineries, and untouched forests. If looking to go off the beaten path and hike or get in touch with nature, Mljet National Park offers scenic forests and tranquil saltwater lakes. Mljet was mentioned in the tale of Odysseus, who remained on Mljet Island for seven years basking in its serene oasis. Greenery and forests cover the majority of the island, while the rest of the island is dotted by fields, vineyards and villages. Mljet Island is also home to remote sandy beaches and the food is incredible. Do we have to go on? With only one hotel on the island, most people visit the island from boat excursions from Korčula or Dubrovnik.

Rab: Best Island to Strip Down to Your Birthday Suit

The area of Rab offers a lot of punch inside its smaller regional area. Rab Town transports you back to the medieval period with historic stone buildings, cobbled streets, impressive Bell Towers and quaint shops while Rab's northern tip, Lopar peninsular offers some of Croatia's best sand beaches. xb Make sure to check the dress code options before your beach trips as some of Rab's most famous beaches such as Kandarola, is purely a European style nudist beach. If you were not to do your research, talk about a grand surprise!

Pag: Where the Beach Parties Are

Although the island was initially known for its delicious Paski sir (Pag cheese), made from sheep's milk, Pag is now better known for its younger demographic and as the best island for beach parties and social gatherings. If you're looking to party with the socials and possibly wonder if you have a liver or not by the end of your stay, Pag should be at the top of your list. After 2007 Zrce beach, near Novalja, is the only place in all of Croatia where bars and clubs are granted 24-hour licenses. In other words, the drinks are constantly flowing all the time. After absorbing the sun and day drinking, locals head to after-beach-parties at the clubs Kalypso, Papaya and Aquarius. These clubs have grown significantly over the years in credibility. Not only do they turn into full-on dance clubs after dark, they've hosted reknown international DJs such as Joe Montana and Tiesto. http://www.pag-tourism.hr

Vis: Best Island to Get Your Wine On

Vis is known for its long history of winegrowing. It's a must-see for wine connoisseurs and fans. Locals and tourists alike know Roki Winery should be at the top of the list. Due to Vis' isolation from growing tourism (it first allowed tourists to visit in 1989), it has kept its remote charm and style of life characteristic of the 1950s. You'll instantly notice that life is a little bit slower on the island of Vis, in the best way. Tourists looking for the "Golden Age of the the Mediterranean as it once was" will find joy when visiting Vis. Transparent clear waters, breathtaking untouched isolated beaches, and historical sights on Vis remind tourists of visits to Monaco or the French Riviera. The isolation has also kept Vis' nature well-preserved nature and ecological essence. The Blue Cave, located off Bisevo Island on Vis, is the area's biggest tourist attraction, and it can be crowded. The blue color of the cave appears when sunlight comes in through a side cave, and it's visible 11 a.m. to noon only on days when the sun shines.

CONCLUSION: AREN'T YOU EXCITED? YOUR TRIP IS ABOUT TO BEGIN!

Thanks for reading the guidebook. We mean it! Your eyes and interest keep us writing these insightful guidebooks, and without you there wouldn't be a reason to creepily lurk from street to street to get the inside scoop.

What was your favorite part about Croatia? Did you head to Hvar the town or Hvar the island for a retreat getaway? Did you head to Pula to visit the amphitheater and compare it's Roman architecture to that of the Coliseum? Which story will be shared for years to come? Was there a meal you'll hopelessly think about and recommend to all who are visiting? Or, was there a moment where you truly felt like a local?

Did our guidebooks help you? We hope you saved some money, laughed at some of our obsessive food comments, and took the time to sip wine and head to an art festival. Did you get lunch at the Outdoor Market in Trznica? What were your thoughts on Croatia's rakia?

Whatever you did in Croatia, we like to think that this guidebook has given you the tools and insightful information to enhance to your tourism experience. As Croatia continues to expand its tourism, it continues to one of the most fashionable places in Europe to visit. Whether backpacking cross-county, beach hopping, or traveling with family, Croatia offers a little something for everyone. Our guide carefully picked both the best tourist and local options to ensure you fully experienced Croatia. Hopefully it showed you the tourist spots you were hoping to see, offered amazing picture opportunities you'll always keep, and the hidden gems that you'll never forget.

We're always looking to improve our guidebooks. If this guidebook wasn't helpful then let us know why or what we can do to make it better. There's no point writing if it's not helpful to travelers and those who experience the guides. We won't take it personally. Furthermore, because this is an electronic book, we know it's not going to end up in the bin. Likewise, if there's something you really liked then we want to know about it.

Thanks again for reading.

Whether you danced the night away and immersed yourself in the nightlife and local cuisine or headed to a remote beach and enjoying nature, we hope you truly enjoyed yourself.

Made in the USA
Lexington, KY
13 December 2017